READ TO ME
Raising Kids
Who Love to Read

READ TO ME
Raising Kids
Who Love to Read

REVISED &
UPDATED

BERNICE E. CULLINAN

SCHOLASTIC INC.

New York   Toronto   London   Auckland   Sydney
Mexico City   New Delhi   Hong Kong   Buenos Aires

Permissions

From "Bedtime" by David L. Harrison.
Copyright © David L. Harrison,
used by permission of Boyds Mills Press.

From *Goodnight Moon* by Margaret Wise Brown.
Copyright © 1947 by Harper and Row Publishers, Inc.
Copyright renewed 1975 by Roberta Brown Rauch.
All rights reserved.
Reprinted by permission of HarperCollins Children's Book.

From "When Grandpa Reads to Me" by John Micklos, Jr.
Copyright © John Micklos, Jr., used by permission.

Cover illustration by Nina Edwards
Cover design by Janet Kusmierski

ISBN 0-439-87399-1

12 11 10 9 8 7 6 5 4 3 2 1   6 7 8 9 10 11/0

Printed in the U.S.A.

To: Kali, Jason, Trisha, Jamison, Haydn
—B.C.

Acknowledgments

This is a family book; it is a book about families written by family members. Many of the experiences are based literally or figuratively on numerous members of our families: Janie and Alan Carley, Marguerite and Webb Ellinger, Bee and Ken Giniger, Dorothy Strickland, Michael and Gweneth Strickland. Thanks to Dr. Beatrice Teitel for the Success Cycle. Thanks to our extended family, Zoya Yusupova and Ernesta Gallo, who care for us regularly.

Dorothy Strickland was my first doctoral student when I began teaching at New York University in 1967–1968. I had been Charlotte Huck's first doctoral student at The Ohio State University; Charlotte proudly called Dorothy her academic grandchild.

We learned to appreciate grandchildren and, during the years, they learned to appreciate us. When our children have children, they realize how much they love them. Then they look back to the past and ask, "Did you love us that much?" The answer is obviously, "Yes." Gradually, as the message sinks in, they say, "Oh, wow. We hadn't realized love was so strong."

This book is dedicated to all of our grandchildren: Kali and Jason Ream; Trisha Carley, Jamison and Haydn Ellinger; Neala and Michaela Strickland; Hannah and Chelsea Strickland; and Cooper and Paige Strickland.

Table of Contents

When Grandpa Reads to Me

I love to climb in Grandpa's lap
To hear my favorite books.
He reads the words and talks about
The pictures as I look.

Adventures flow from every page
When Grandpa reads the tales
Of pirates roaming on the seas
And ships with golden sails.

The characters can spring to life
Like Peter Pan and Pooh,
Madeline and Curious George
And Peter Rabbit, too.

Grandpa even does the voices.
I laugh until I'm weak
When I hear Grandpa's deep, low voice
Do Piglet's high-pitched squeak.

There's nothing I can't do through books.
There's nothing I can't see.
The whole world opens up its arms
When Grandpa reads to me.

Foreword

A nine-month-old girl coos to her grandmother as she is being readied for bed. Grandma talks to the baby about her pretty blanket, the nice bath, and what a beautiful child she is. She sits the baby on her lap and opens a familiar book of lullabies. They look at the pictures as Grandma sings. Now and then, Grandma pauses and the child sings in her own special way. They seem to take turns as the book sharing and singing continue.

Board books with thick pages are the favorites of a two-year-old who reads with Mom and Dad, to her infant sister, or on her own. With books she knows well, she takes great delight in finding and placing her whole hand on a picture as her parents call out the name of each object.

Big sister loves to play patty-cake, sing chants, and read rhyming books with her baby sister, imitating what she has seen her parents do. Sometimes the family laughs when baby sister is heard attempting to "read" them on her own as she plays alone.

A seven-year-old girl and her mom share a wide variety of books — picture books, chapter books, books of poetry, and informational books — just to name a few. They approach them differently, however. Picture storybooks are read all at once. Chapter books are read over time and so are informational books, because they sometimes stop and talk about certain pages for a very long time. Sometimes they only select two or three poems to be read from a poetry book. They borrowed a book of recipes for children from the library and plan to make cupcakes.

Informational books are the favorites of this eleven-year-old boy. He is fond of interesting and unusual facts — the more bizarre the better. He and his father talk a lot about what they read. Sometimes Dad asks, "What do you think is happening here and what makes you think so?" or "What do you think will happen next?" Sometimes he reminisces about experiences he has had like those in the book — "Remember when . . ."

These vignettes are based on experiences from my own family. However, they are typical of many other families that I know well. They illustrate the power of sharing books with children. They also demonstrate key concepts underlying shared book experiences, for example, the importance of: (1) providing time for reading to children and talking with them about what is read; (2) using the shared book experience to stimulate conversations about ideas and concepts that sometimes go well beyond everyday experiences; (3) including a variety of types of literature, such as informational books and poetry, as well as story books; (4) making books accessible for children to return to on their own to read or to "pretend read" — a child's personal reenactment of the read-aloud experience.

Reading to and with children for the affective benefits is valuable in and of itself. But story time is a value-added endeavor. Its worth in the literacy development of young children is undisputed. For many years, researchers have known that shared book experiences play an important role in helping young children get off to a good start in reading. Invariably, the child who learns to read before receiving formal instruction or the one who is primed and ready to read at the onset of formal instruction has been read to on a regular basis at home. This is true of children regardless of where they live, their home language, their ethnic background, or their family's income level. That is a very powerful message and one that researchers could not resist studying to find out why something so informal and pleasurable could also be such an important source of learning. They learned several things.

One of the most important outcomes of sharing books with children is that parent and child share a joyful and intimate experience involving books and reading. This builds positive attitudes, an absolute must if learning to read is to occur. The benefits of story time go well beyond support for the affective "feelings" of children, however. Story time has a profound effect on a child's language and cognitive development, as well. Without a lesson plan or script, parents instinctively expand on what they read in order to help clarify ideas; they explain new vocabulary and concepts, and they engage in rich discussions about content that help to build background knowledge. Since parents know their child best, it is easy for them to relate the content of a book to what the child already knows and has experienced.

My hope, of course, is that every young child would have the benefit of these important experiences with a parent or caregiver. In *Read to Me: Raising Kids Who Love to Read*, Bernice Cullinan provides us with an excellent, easy-to-use resource to make that happen. I can think of no better gift for children and those who care for them.

Dorothy S. Strickland,
Samuel DeWitt Proctor Professor of Education
Rutgers, The State University of New Jersey

Chapter 1: Raising Readers

Dear Mom,
You did so many things for me when I was growing up. Maybe the ones I remember best seemed pretty ordinary to you — like reading to me every night in bed. I remember thinking that Curious George had more fun than I did even though he got in trouble. And Dr. Seuss taught me what loyalty was when Horton sat on those eggs to hatch them. Henry Huggins and Nancy Drew seemed like kids down the street. You made me feel important and loved with everything you did. For all the times I forgot to tell you then, thanks, Mom.
Janie

Years ago, my daughter sent this card to me on my birthday. It remains one of my favorite all-time gifts and reminds me that reading aloud works its magic in both directions — from the parent to the child and then back, double-fold, to the parent. I experienced that magic as I read to my own children and have passed the magic along to them as they have become parents.

My daughter-in-law, Marguerite, has shared her experiences with reading to her sons (my grandchildren) over the years:

As a parent, you fall back on what you know, and being a bookworm from an early age, I have surrounded my two boys with books. There are books in the kitchen, living room, car, bedrooms. Books have been the most valuable tool I have been able to find to provide us with peaceful dinners in restaurants, quiet times for snuggling, answers to the myriad questions we get on a daily basis, and for subtly illustrating concepts that I want them to understand. I don't know when they will become readers on their own, but I hope books are something we will always share together.

Reading to each of my two boys is a very individual experience. Jamison, who is six, is passionate about informational books. It almost doesn't matter the subject: the solar system, knights, insects, dinosaurs, buildings. He is so full of questions about the world that it is a challenge to get through each page while fielding all of his inquiries. Haydn, who is four, adores stories. Once the book is finished, he will immediately insist on taking a turn "reading" it back to me. Clearly, reading to both of them demands patience, but the rewards are great!

As Jamison gets older, he increasingly wants to create his own stories. Though only five, he came to me the other day with a picture of a boy that he had drawn and proudly declared: "This is my character. How do you spell "He likes to eat chocolate?" Sometimes Jamison will draw the pictures and dictate the words to me, as in the story "The Adventures of Super Fast Hot Race Car Wheels."

Marguerite grew up in a reading family. Naturally, she created an environment for her own family as "readers" — she brought stacks of her own books. She had worked in a publishing house meeting deadlines, editing, proofreading, creating headlines, and writing editorials before she and my son Webb decided to have children. When their first child, Jamison, was born, he was surrounded by books and people ready and willing to read to him endlessly. Three years later, Haydn was born. There were not as many volunteers to read, but certainly even more books spilled from bookcases and cartons. The two boys have many books to keep them engaged.

My years as a teacher, mother, and grandmother have shown me firsthand what loving to read does for a child. Children who are read to are confident, alert, and in charge of their world. They don't need to depend on others to do their thinking for them; they can find out what they want to know by themselves. The feelings of independence and self-esteem make a marked difference in children assuming responsibility for their actions and in their attitudes toward life.

Classic children's literature may be timeless in the joy and wonder it inspires, but I decided this book could use an update. The world continues to change at breathtaking speed. We have discovered more about children's mental growth; new research on the brain shows surprising developments at an earlier age than previously thought. There is more technology available in the home, school, and library. The workplace is being constantly reinvented. Our homes feature more single working parents, more multicultural families, and more participation by fathers in parenting activities. This edition is an attempt to catch up with today's children (who, as you parents know, are always on the move). With more technological bells and whistles competing for our children's time and attention, we need to make sure they slow down long enough to learn and to appreciate the value and fun of reading. And that's what this book is about.

"Please read to me" is more than a child's request for attention; it's an opportunity to expand a child's mind. The joy flows in both directions, so be prepared to enjoy the process yourself.

Raising a child is the most important job you'll ever tackle. It's also the most demanding: You work at it twenty-four hours a day, you get no vacations, you can never retire, and you don't get paid a nickel. Attempts to form an international parents' union to address these issues seem destined for failure — just try to find any two parents who can agree on how to raise a child.

Still, you do your best and you take your job seriously. You buy warm clothes for your child. You get sneakers that are the right size and offer good support for growing feet. You make sure your child wears a helmet for in-line skating or bike riding. You make sure your child has proper rest and eats healthy food. But what about your child's mind — are you feeding the imagination? Are you feeding that endless curiosity that causes young children's minds to grow in healthy ways?

It seems as if you answer a hundred of your child's questions every day and you know you will continue to answer lots more. But you can't possibly have all the answers all the time. You want to make your child independent. Your child needs to learn from other sources — especially from books. Books are an endless treasury of knowledge . . . and pleasure. And with your help, your child can discover the wonderful world of books and become an enthusiastic lifelong reader. If you teach your children to love to read, you are handing down a special kind of magic to them — a gift that will enrich their lives as nothing else can do. You'll reap some unexpected bonuses, too.

Your children will:

- Improve as readers

- Do better in school
- Gain confidence
- Become more independent
- Appreciate a larger, richer world

And you will:

- Take extreme pleasure in watching your children become readers
- Enjoy favorite stories from your childhood
- Discover new books written since you were a child
- Have more free time while your child reads alone

You may say, "But I don't know how to teach my child to read. That's the school's job." Certainly, the school has a very important role to play and will spend many years developing reading skills, but you have the most important, most continuous, and most lasting influence on your child as a reader! The school needs you as a partner; your continued support over the years makes a lasting difference.

Some very simple things you do now will have a big payoff in the years to come. For example, you can say, "Come here and look at this book I'm reading. It tells about some wonderful children's books we can read together. Let's see if we can find one that sounds good to you." Letting your child know that you are interested in her books tells her that reading is important to you. Even more crucial, it tells her that *she* is important to you. Asking her to find books she likes shows that you want her to enjoy reading; it tells her reading is not a chore but something to enjoy. It is the beginning of many happy hours spent sharing books.

Yes, raising a child is the most important and demanding job you'll ever tackle. So what can you expect from this lifetime labor? Just the reward that comes from watching your children grow into loving, responsible, competent human beings. And for a bonus, how about a lifetime of appreciation for the help you gave them? And years of fun. And the likelihood that the people you live with will be more interesting, more interested, and better companions. And remember — being a child is no easy job, either. You're on this journey together. Take some books along.

How to Use This Book

This is a self-help book intended to make life easier for you. The book is divided into three major sections. The first section (Chapters 1 and 2) shows that when children learn to read they need the same kinds of conditions they needed to learn to talk. The strong connections between reading and writing are first explored here; they are extended in later sections.

The second section (Chapters 3 and 4) is packed with practical hands-on ideas. The chapters contain numerous tips *from* busy parents *for* busy parents who need to find information quickly. Feel free to turn to those pages first to pick up some immediate pointers on surrounding children with books and developing a love of reading.

Section three (Chapters 5 through 9) is divided by age groups. In these age-related chapters you will find features to explain what reading and writing looks like for each developmental stage. The chapters begin with a list of observable characteristics of children (things to watch for) as they relate to reading and writing activities. Each chapter features children of that age, to show how reading and writing fit into that child's daily life. The chapters cite topics that most children are interested in and give specific reading tips for each age.

In this book, we suggest activities that lead children to read and ways to keep them reading. General tips appropriate for any age child appear in Chapter 4; activities that work best for a specific age group appear in the age-related chapters. For example, the suggestion "You read to me and I'll read to you" is in the chapter for beginning readers. "Read one character's speaking part" appears for older children who are well along their way in knowing how to read.

Every child will, of course, mature and develop individual skills at his or her own pace. These age-related chapters provide generalized information about children of each age group. If the section on six-year-olds doesn't accurately describe your six-year-old, you might find the discussion of five-year-olds or the chapter on seven-year-olds more appropriate.

The special feature "Did You Know . . ." contains interesting tidbits and pieces of information related to children's reading and writing. These bits and pieces of information often point out how children's activities at home relate to their performance at school.

When you go into a library or bookstore or see a book club offering, you see hundreds of books and you want to make good choices. A list at the end of this book contains books too good to miss for each age level.

You're on your way! You have decided that you want to make reading important to your child. You purchased this book and you're ready to go! You will find it to be one of the most rewarding experiences of your life. Nurturing a reader is like nurturing a garden. It takes effort and diligence, but it's fun, healthy work — and the flowers that blossom are worth the effort. Enjoy the planting.

How Children Learn Language

A Hispanic father and his three-year-old son were playing at the neighborhood swimming pool. The boy stood at the edge of the pool ready to jump into the water and into his father's protective arms. Their conversation went something like this:

> Dad: Are you ready to dive into the pool?
> Boy: Yes.
> Dad: Well, say it.
> Boy: I'm ready to dive into the pool.
> Dad: Are you positively sure you're ready to dive into the pool?
> Boy: I'm positively sure I'm ready to dive into the pool.
> Dad: Are you absolutely positively sure you're ready to dive into the pool?
> Boy: I'm absolutely positively sure I'm ready to dive into the pool.
> Dad: Are you absolutely positively certain you're ready to dive into the pool?
> Boy: I'm absolutely positively certain I'm ready to dive into the pool.
> Dad: Well, go ahead then.

SPLASH! Later the father sang songs and recited rhymes to the child and encouraged him to make up his own. The father spoke to the child in a normal conversational tone; there was no baby talk, no condescension. The boy asked about swimming in the ocean. The father explained the difference between swimming in a pool and swimming in the ocean. Among other contrasts, he pointed out that we could hurt the sea animals by swimming in the ocean.

The boy returned to the edge of the pool for another jump and this time his father counted out loud in English, Spanish, and French — "One, two, three; *uno, dos, tres; un, deux, trois*" — as the child repeated the numbers and then leaped, squealing with laughter. The father was not only having a delicious time bonding with his son, he was expanding his child's language, teaching him vocabulary and a means of expression that extended far beyond the swimming lesson.

You are your child's first and most important teacher. And take some credit: You are a highly successful teacher. You've already taught one of the most complex and difficult disciplines imaginable — spoken language. You taught your child to talk, to listen, and to understand words. You probably say, "Oh, but they learn that naturally." But if a hungry child raised by wolves crept into your kitchen on all fours, she might growl or whine, but she probably wouldn't say, "May I please have some peanut butter?" Your child needed your help to learn to talk; from the beginning, you provided certain learning conditions.

For example, from the very moment your child came into your home, you surrounded her with language. You talked to her while you were feeding her. You talked to her while you were dressing her. You talked to her while you were bathing her. You never stopped talking! We immerse children in words as we fill their every waking moment with the sounds of our language. Even though we say, "Well, I know she can't understand me," we keep on talking.

Just as you surrounded your child with talk, now you need to surround your child with reading and writing. It's amazing to realize, but if you do the same things you did when your child was learning to talk, he can learn to read and to write with pretty much the same ease. Similar conditions that help a child learn the skills of spoken language help him learn the skills of written language. Let's look at some of these conditions.

At some very early point, your child tried to imitate you by making sounds himself. You were his model and, by talking, you provided him with a model of what talking sounds like. When he first tried to talk, his attempts didn't sound a whole lot like your model but you praised the effort. If he said "wa-wa," you gave him a drink of water. You didn't scold him and say, "No, say wa-ter." When he first said "Mama" or "Dada," you really praised the attempt! You called your mother or the neighbor and had him say it again and again so that everybody could hear. We praise children for being nearly right when they first try to say words. When my granddaughter Trisha started saying, "Nank-oo," we all smiled and said, "You're welcome."

You also serve as his model when you read aloud to him. You show how a person reads a book: You hold the book upright, you read the title, you turn the pages, you look at the words. As you read, you demonstrate what reading sounds like. Similarly, any time you write something down, your child is watching and learning from your model. Not surprisingly, your child will start to imitate you. His initial attempts at reading and writing may seem clumsy, but they are no more "wrong" than a child who starts out saying "goo-goo" and progresses to "wa-wa." And if we praise the child's first efforts at reading and writing without criticism or correction, we encourage his progress.

In talking to your child you demonstrated what talking sounds like and also what it means. You showed your child what language is by demonstrating what it does. Your child gradually attached meanings to the words she heard and began to try to say them to express those meanings. "Goo-goo" might be just an experiment in sound, but "wa-wa" is talk with a purpose. Your child learned that she could use language to get others to respond — to give her a drink of water or a hug. Children learn that talking gets things done that they want to accomplish; spoken language makes things happen. It has meaning in their lives. Since they want to be in charge of their world they will try it, too.

What Do We Mean by "Reading"?

Before we continue, we need to be clear about what we mean by "reading." Put simply, reading is getting meaning from print. There is nothing simple about the process, but the idea is simple enough. In the same way that a child learns to speak words for their meaning, a child learns to read for the meaning of the words. Meaning, as it is coded into language, is the reason for talking and for reading. It may seem logical to want to break words down into their smallest elements — sounds and letters — to learn to read. But we don't do this with talking and there is little reason for parents to do it with beginning reading. We may talk or read more slowly with a beginner, but tiny pieces of language are more abstract and more difficult to learn than meaningful chunks of language. There are reasons for a child eventually to develop the ability to break a word into its separate sounds — to recognize rhyming words or to distinguish beginning sounds, for instance, as his appreciation for the subtleties of writing grows. But if you read to your child regularly, he will develop this awareness on his own. Research shows that familiarity with nursery rhymes is excellent for all facets of children's reading development.

The child's instinct to derive meaning from language does not mean that the sounds of words are unimportant. The music of language is one of its great joys, and one of its most powerful attractions for children. Poems are especially entertaining for children because the words rhyme and are fun to say. Verses encourage children to bounce around while saying the words. The words match the rhythm of a child's movements; the rhythm underscores the words' meanings. Read the same poems to your children over and over again; you'll soon hear familiar phrases fall trippingly from their tongues.

Here are a few of the first things your child learns to do when he watches you read:

- Hold a book right side up
- Turn to the front of the book to begin
- Turn pages at the appropriate time when the story is being read
- Point to words instead of pictures when reading
- Pick out a favorite book from a shelf of books

These are book-handling skills and are often used to assess young children's readiness to learn to read. (They are also used to determine maturity level for entrance to school.) These beginning steps in the process of learning to read are discussed in more detail in the age-related chapters that follow.

Writing Is Connected to Reading

Reading and writing go hand in hand. Reading words that make sense and writing down words with children show them that these two activities are connected parts of the same process, two sides of the same coin. Writing shows a child that anything he says can be put into print; that it can be read back now or later; that talking, writing, and reading are all connected to meaning. There are lots of things in this area that you can do to reinforce these connections. Here are a few for younger children:

Show your child a letter from Grandma. Point to the spot that says the child's name (surely Grandma used it). Have your child dictate a message she wants to tell Grandma while you write it down. Let your child sign her name. Mail the letter. Maybe the return mail will bring another letter to your child.

Give your child paper and markers so he can make pictures and write words and letters. Tape them onto the refrigerator to show off his work and your pride in it.

Write your shopping list for the grocery store in front of your child. Say the sounds of the words as you write them; exaggerate the sounds of the letters — *Mmmmm* as you write the letter "M." Ask your child to show you where it says "milk" or "bread." Use a word that starts with a consonant. Vowels are more difficult to distinguish. Let her copy words from boxes and cans in the kitchen. When you're at the grocery store, ask her to help find the items on the list.

Reading Is for All People, All Times, and All Places

Whatever your background, your reading level, or your occupation, there are books for you and your children. If you speak Italian, read to them in Italian. If you speak Spanish, read to them in Spanish. Books in the lists at the end of this book are available in other languages; choose the version that's best for your child. Books representing different cultures reinforce a child's heritage and help build self-esteem. But no matter what the language, we *must* read to our children.

Eighty-two percent of prison inmates are school dropouts and 60 percent are illiterate. Barbara's job was to teach the women inmates of Cell Block 14 how to read. She had started out trying to conduct a basic adult literacy class, but nobody seemed interested. She tried to make the classes more relevant and practical by bringing in job application forms, résumé outlines, and fashion magazines. Nobody cared. Finally, Barbara coaxed it out of one woman that she would like to learn to read in order to read stories to her young daughter.

Next day, Barbara brought in an armload of children's books to her prison classroom — books with easy patterned language and vivid illustrations; books with nursery rhymes, jump-rope rhymes, and simple poems; books with photographs of objects and a single word on a page. Suddenly, the women inmates, many of whom had children, were intrigued. The thought of learning to read for the sake of their kids overcame any embarrassment they may have felt, and Barbara's class became popular and the students enthusiastic. Barbara started each class by reading aloud from one of the books, and the women worked hard to have something new to read each time their children came to see them; they worked to stay one step ahead of the next visit.

Reading aloud is one of the most useful secrets you'll ever find for being an effective parent: It soothes a sick child, calms a fearful one, and eases a fretful one into sleep. Tommy, the son of one of my friends, had to have tubes put in his ears as the result of repeated ear infections. Fear of the unknown made Tommy especially tense and uncooperative. After reading a story several times about Coco Bear, who had tubes put in his ears, Tommy faced the simple procedure bravely.

Dorothy Butler, a bookstore owner in New Zealand, tells about her grandchild, Cushla, who was a multihandicapped, chronically ill baby. Even though doctors said Cushla would have problems in school, her parents read books aloud to her to while away long hours in hospitals and doctors' offices. Despite her severe problems, at age six and a half, Cushla was reading alone at a level far above her actual age. Her parents had made books and language a vital part of her life, and

Cushla had fooled the doctors and learned to read, despite dire predictions that she would not.

Books can help you as a parent in many family situations. When a new baby is coming along, books that deal with that situation head-on help a child express deep inner fears of being replaced or unloved when the newcomer arrives. Books can ease concerns about losing a tooth, having an operation, serving as a flower girl in a wedding, or facing parents' divorce. A child can learn how a character in a book deals with peer pressure. There is a backward and forward flow between books and what happens in real life. Children use real-life experiences to help them understand books and books help them understand real life.

We never know exactly what is going to appeal to a child, so don't be too selective in choosing books. If your child loves toy trucks, try to find books about trucks. If he is interested in the stars, find some books on astronomy or sky watching. If she wants to be an astronaut, get her books about astronauts and space travel.

Telling stories to children is important, too. After all, it is the stories in books that make them so appealing to a child. We have an instant audience when we say, "Let me tell you about when I was a little girl."

My son once said, "Mommy, tell me about the olden days when they had covered wagons and pioneers when you were a little girl." The time frame may have been a little off, but I appreciated his interest. Stories about the good old days give children a sense of their family heritage. Do you remember some of the stories your parents or relatives told you? Isn't it fun to hear the one about how Aunt Emily nibbled like a mouse to eat chunks of icing off the pineapple upside-down cake while the rest of the family was out in the barn milking the cows?

Do you remember stories that you loved hearing as a child? Tell them to your children. You can edit out parts they might not understand — or parts you don't want them to understand! I told many stories about my little sister in which I took liberties to add to her misbehavior; Aunt Doty stories were ones my children asked for repeatedly. The stories you tell become part of your child's storehouse of experience; they keep the past alive so that the memories can be passed down from generation to generation.

Chapter 2: Why Reading to Your Child Matters

You may have tangible wealth untold:
Caskets of jewels and coffers of gold.
Richer than I you can never be —
I had a mother who read to me.
From "The Reading Mother" by Strickland Gillilan

One of my young neighbors, with children ages eight, six, and four years old, said, "Thank goodness Brendan is reading by himself now so I don't have to read to him anymore." My neighbor is wrong about that! She is depriving her child — and herself — of a unique and precious opportunity. Even though eight-year-old Brendan is able to read alone, he still needs to have his parents read to him. Even if a teacher reads to Brendan at school or the local librarian reads aloud during story hour, those group experiences, though valuable, can't compare to hearing a story read aloud by his own mother or father at home. The experiences are totally different. When *you* read to your children, you are teaching them much more than just the material you are reading.

When a child sits close to his mother as she reads, he is reassured that he's still important to her — even though, as in Brendan's case, younger siblings may have invaded his space. What the mother or father is telling the child in clear, unspoken language is, "We spend time with you because we care about you. You are safe and secure; we will always protect you." All children need to hear these messages; reading together is a good way to tell them. Reading aloud establishes a close, loving bond between a parent and a child that can be forged in no better way.

When you read aloud to your child, she uses what she

hears to make sense of her world and to understand what is happening around her. Your child learns more than just stories. Books become a jumping-off place for a child and parent to talk about real-life experiences and to clarify questions in a relaxed, personal way that could never happen in a group reading at school or at the library.

As you read a book, the story and the conversation it inspires trigger memories from your life that you can share with your child. Your story then reminds your child of something similar that happened to her just last week. And the exchange continues as we talk about a story long after the reading is over. We relate events from the story to everyday life, saying, for example, "Today is just like Alexander's terrible, horrible, no good, very bad day," after Judith Viorst's book of the same title, or "You're just like the little engine that could — just keep saying, 'I think I can, I think I can.'" The family develops its own references, its own special language.

When you read aloud, your child discovers something else that is precious — a wonderful side of you that you might keep hidden much of the time. Juan Arroyo may be an imposing-looking police lieutenant by day, but in the evening, with a book in hand and his daughter, Carmen, on his lap, Lieutenant Arroyo magically becomes a timid grasshopper. To her coworkers, Dorothy Poplowski is a no-nonsense bank manager, but when she reads to her son, Daniel, she can be an orchestra of animal sounds. Being a grown-up calls for much control and discipline. Occasionally, you have to be stern with your children and you may feel terrible about it. After all, you can remember when you were a kid. Reading aloud gives you permission, in fact makes a demand on you, to drop the grown-up mask, relax, and be that kid again yourself.

Your children will always remember the special things you gave them when they were young. Books should be among their childhood memories. If they have warm memories of cuddling with a parent and a good story, they associate those happy feelings with reading as they strike out to read alone. The feelings remain long after the stories are forgotten.

At the beginning of this chapter, Brendan's mother speaks of reading to her son as if it were a chore. We can only guess that this mother wasn't read to as a child, that she didn't develop those warm lifetime memories. If so, it's not too late; she and Brendan can start a new family tradition. Reading aloud becomes part of your family heritage. If you read to your children, they will read to theirs. It's as simple as that. Children learn more from what we do than from what we say. They learn what we value. The things they learn become lasting memories. If you make books an important part of your family's life, your children will remember the books, the stories, and the warm cozy times you spent sharing them. When they grow up, they will share the same things with their children. One day, my daughter, Janie said, "Mom, when you read to us, I just took it for granted. Now that I have my own children, I find that I'm doing the same thing. It's sort of like handing down the magic." We are handing down the magic of reading, imagination, and thinking when we pass on our love of books. It's a torch passed from one generation to the next.

Reading Aloud to Your Child

Reading aloud helps in many ways. It:

- Establishes bonds of love
- Opens doors
- Becomes part of family heritage
- Is fun
- Builds the desire to read

- Gives educational advantage
- Develops the ability to read alone

Joe, father of Eileen, Kerry, and Brian, had a special way of announcing to his children that it was time for their bedtime story. He would sit on the couch, spread his arms wide, and say, "The gates are closing . . . the gates-s-s-s . . . are . . . clo-o-o-o . . . sing" as he slowly closed the big circle of his arms for the nightly reading session. The children rushed to get ready for bed and to get inside the circle of arms that snapped closed when all three were safely inside. Eileen ran like crazy to get inside the circle; it seemed like a matter of life and death to her. She recalls with pleasure the memories of stories told and books read inside the closed gates.

There are many good reasons for reading aloud to your child. But one of the best reasons is that it's fun. Reading aloud is enjoyable because the stories themselves are fun — not only for your child listener but for you, the adult reader. Authors think about the adults who read their stories to young children when they are writing them; they put in little jokes or subtle comments for the adults to appreciate. J. K. Rowling does not blunt her pen when writing for children; she uses a rich vocabulary and timeless story line that appeals to adults as well as children in *Harry Potter and the Sorcerer's Stone* and subsequent titles in the series. In *Owen*, Kevin Henkes winks knowingly at the adult reader when he has a neighbor say, "Don't you think he's a little old to be carrying a blanket?"

Outstanding illustrators consistently add details to their art that call for repeated viewing. Ed Young hides a mouse on each page of *Cats Are Cats*. Chris Van Allsburg hides his dog, Fritz, among the art in his picture books as in *Jumanji* and *The Garden of Abdul Gasazi*. You and your child find new things to talk about in the story and illustrations each time you reread a book. This is an unexpected pleasure of reading aloud: It's fun for you as well as your child.

Another reason reading aloud is fun is the remarkably high quality of the books you read. The world's finest artists, writers, and poets contribute to children's books. The result: Children's books are more beautiful, more imaginative, better written than ever before. In some make-believe storybooks, spiders weave words into webs, pigs talk, and a frog plays tricks on a toad. One of my neighbors explained, "I feel like a whole new world has opened up to me. I haven't even looked at kids' books since I was a child and I didn't pay much attention to them then. The only ones I read were Nancy Drew. I had no idea there were so many different kinds available — and they're beautiful!" Some of the very best writing today can be found in children's books.

You make reading aloud more fun if, as you read, you speak in the voice of the characters. For *Goldilocks and the Three Bears*, use Papa Bear's gruff, growly voice, Mama Bear's middle-sized voice, and Baby Bear's tiny, squeaky voice. Even more fun, playact the story with everybody taking parts. Children are always ready to playact the parts of favorite stories. The first time you act out a story, assign parts that are fitting, that is, Dad could be Papa Bear, Mom could be Mama Bear, and the child, Baby Bear. After you've done it this way a few times, reverse the roles so that your child plays Papa Bear. The whole game gets even more hilarious as you mix up the roles. It also helps to develop a creative imagination, a necessary component of a twenty-first-century mind.

Likewise, read books in a tone that conveys their meaning. If a book is deliciously funny and silly, read it in a silly voice. If it's somber and sad, use a more serious tone. Most of all, have fun while you read — and share the fun with your child.

Your child is such a great audience you may even discover

unknown talents in yourself. Ron had always been too shy to sing until he became a new parent. When he started singing lullabies to his baby daughter, he discovered that he liked singing and that, surprisingly, he had a pretty good voice. Ron now sings with his town's community chorus.

Reading aloud to your child at home helps establish the idea that reading is something a person does for himself, for his own enjoyment, in the comfort of his own home. If all reading takes place at a day care center, at school, or at a library, a child may see reading as an activity that only happens at an institution of some sort under more formal conditions.

Reading aloud to your child builds the desire to read for both of you. Children learn that exciting stories come from books and that reading is worth the effort. When we read children's stories as adults, they allow us to get in touch with the child inside us. Both parents and children enjoy the imaginative stories, engaging illustrations, and lilting language found in today's children's books. Reading aloud may even inspire you to pick up that novel you've been wanting to read. *Harry Potter and the Sorcerer's Stone* and its sequels by J. K. Rowling sparked a reading phenomenon unparalleled in the United States. The Harry Potter books have continued to hold the top spots on *The New York Times* best seller list for years. Adults enjoy the books as much as children do. I stood in line at midnight to get my own copy of the most recent title!

Reading to your child provides a valuable educational advantage; there's no better way to achieve it. Children who are read to do far better in school than those who are not. Children are sponges. They soak up everything they see and hear. When they hear stories they love, they remember endless details and learn things we are not even aware they are learning.

Young readers comprehend words they hear more quickly

than words they see; these processes are established early but seem to reverse sometime during the teenage years. Until middle school, most children are better at listening than they are at reading. Therefore, you can choose books for reading aloud that are a bit above their reading level; if they don't understand something, you are right there to explain it. By doing this, you encourage them to read books that inch them up a notch in their reading level.

A child is less able to understand a word she comes across in reading that she has never heard. Understanding new words in spoken language helps a child understand them while reading. If a child has never heard the word *earthquake* she is not likely to recognize it or readily understand what it means when she faces it in a book. She certainly will not use it in her writing. But she will learn the meaning of the word from hearing you read about it and talk about it. In fact, vocabulary grows more from reading than from any other activity.

I recently watched David Harrison read some of his poetry to a New York City fourth-grade class. When he finished, he asked if there were any questions. The kids did *not* ask, "Where do you get your ideas?" or "Are you married?" They asked, "What's a gravel bar?" and "What's a snake stick?" — references to terms David had used in his poems about growing up in the Midwest, terms that were unfamiliar to these city kids. Children build a storehouse of words from hearing books read aloud; they draw upon these words and their meanings when they read and write on their own. Choose books above their reading level when reading aloud; you'll be expanding their vocabularies.

Written language is not the same as spoken language. One important reason reading aloud gives children an educational advantage is what they automatically pick up about written language as they listen. We use different words, different kinds of sentences, and different punctuation to express meaning. Children notice all these things as you read aloud, especially if they sit beside you and can see the page as you read. What they see and hear make written language easier for them to understand when they read alone.

No matter how much your child reads alone, it's still important for you to read aloud to him. Remember the models and demonstrations you gave your child to learn to talk. He needs models for reading, too. He needs to hear what reading sounds like when it is done by a competent reader. Teacher Kathy Harwood decided to read aloud to her struggling sixth-grade students in New York City. Most of them had never been read to before, had never heard what good reading sounded like. She gave every student a copy of the book she was reading so they could follow along. The students admitted that, as they listened, they would sometimes get caught up in the story and "sneak-read ahead" to find out what was going to happen next, a stark contrast to their previous difficulties in comprehension when reading one — word — at — a — time. They also said that when they read the book on their own, they could hear the sound of Kathy's voice in their ears.

Reading aloud contributes to a child's ability to read alone. This happens gradually for many children who sit on a parent's lap to listen and watch the reader's finger move across the page pointing to the words as they are read. This happens best for beginning readers if the material you read is patterned, repetitive, rhythmic, and rhymed. Children continually try to make sense of their world; they search for patterns to explain the way things work. Patterns in spoken language and print help them learn to read.

Early readers make connections between the sounds of words and the beginning letters or end rhymes of words. You don't need to give your child flash cards and isolated letters of the alphabet! You do need to point to the words as you read. And you do need to answer a child's questions. Tell him the names and sounds of the letters when he asks. Emphasize the sounds of initial consonants. Ask him to find other words on the page that start with the same letter. Children are interested in their names. Use your child's name to teach letter recognition.

Two major ingredients in instilling a love of reading are the right book and the time to share it with your child. Gordon Wells calls children "meaning makers" — they use language as their most powerful tool for organizing what they know. Knowing and feeling are bound together in a child's mind. The poet David Harrison expresses this double meaning in a child's request for a bedtime story:

> "Read me a story,
> Please read me to sleep."
> "But what kind of story, my dear?"
> "Read any story
> And I'll go to sleep,
> As long as I know you are near."
> — 1996

Reading Alone

Reading alone helps in many ways. It:

- Develops independence
- Expands a child's world
- Increases self-esteem
- Stirs the imagination
- Establishes lifelong reading habits

- Develops vocabulary
- Develops understanding of other people

Reading is one of the most liberating things we can do. In fact, before the Civil War, slave owners were so aware of the liberating power of reading that slaves were not allowed to learn how to read. Reading made them unfit for slavery. Frederick Douglass, an American abolitionist and son of a black slave, lived from 1817 to 1895. He learned to read in secret and passed his secret to many others. Reading became the pathway to freedom; it still is.

Reading alone helps a child develop independence. One of our goals as parents is to help children do things on their own. Reading alone helps a child to become independent as a learner. She can search for facts alone, entertain herself alone, and expand her horizons alone — if she reads. Reading paves the road to independence.

Reading alone expands a child's world. He can be transported to other times and other places through reading. He can see what it was like to sail across the ocean on the *Mayflower* or to live in North America during the early settlement of Plymouth Colony. History textbooks give facts, but historical stories have the power to make him feel as if he were living in a pioneer settlement. Through reading, he can imagine life in the future or on a distant planet. Books help him consider the impossible and realize the many choices he has in life.

Reading allows us to live more lives than the one we have. We can face fear and loneliness without leaving the safety of our homes. We can sail around the world without fear of shipwreck or suffer blindness without loss of sight, while still probing the emotions of the moment. We can rehearse experiences we might have someday: We can find a friend, or lose one, or climb a mountain in the Himalayas. Books cannot replace real-life experiences, but they do help us decide which experiences are worth seeking. Of course, it's easier on the parents, too, that their child can take his earliest journeys on the living room couch. He'll be going off on real adventures soon enough.

Children sometimes act as if they need to be entertained all the time. They want to have friends around, or have the TV on, or be in the thick of some activity. In our increasingly fast-paced culture, reading is an excellent way for children to increase their attention spans and develop patience. Children who learn to read alone and love it can entertain themselves; they spend time alone happily. They are the ones who curl up with a book. Readers seem to have a good sense of themselves. They are comfortable with themselves and enjoy being quiet and reading. This type of independence will serve them well for their whole lives.

Reading stirs the imagination — that ability to make-believe and to imagine things that do not yet exist. Space travel would not be a reality if it had not been imagined first. Reading helps to create scenes in our minds that we might never see without the vivid words on a page. Reading builds a sense of wonder.

Reading alone establishes reading as a lifelong habit. It also makes children better readers because they get good at what they practice. For example, if you practice playing the piano a lot, you get better at it. As you get better, you are willing to practice more. The more you practice, the better you get — and it becomes more fun. In reading, like so many other things, practice makes perfect. I call it a Success Cycle. It is a cycle we want to get children into as readers. The more you read, the better you read. The better you read, the more you enjoy it. The more you enjoy it, the more you want to read.

Reading independently improves reading fluency — the ability to read with speed, accuracy, and comprehension.

Reading increases a child's vocabulary. Children are word collectors — they grab hold of interesting new words and make them their own. The more words a child knows, the better she will be able to read. Through reading, children discover the meaning of many words they would never come across in ordinary talk simply because people use words in books they don't use in speaking. For example, a book will state "she replied," but you seldom hear anyone say that. Children can often figure out the meaning of an unfamiliar word in a book from its context, the words surrounding the new word. Knowing what words mean is a big help, in fact,

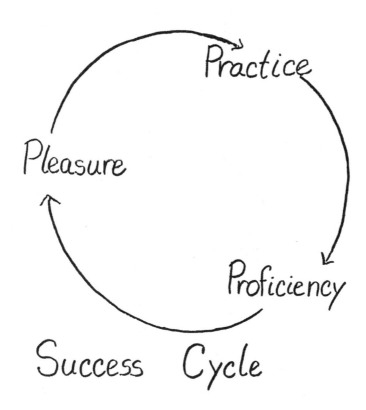

a requirement, of knowing how to read them. It works both ways: We need to know a word before we can read it, but reading helps us learn the new word.

Reading helps us to understand other people, their customs, and their cultures. We can walk in another's shoes and feel what it's like to live inside another's life when we read something written from that person's point of view. We can understand life in historical times when we experience it through a historical novel.

Good writers describe people and situations so vividly we think we are there as we read. For example, we shiver from the icy blasts of wind as we read about the Little Match Girl and we feel isolation and rejection as we read about the Ugly Duckling. When Homer Price cannot turn off a doughnut machine, we laugh but feel sympathy for him as he tries to find a place to put all the doughnuts that keep popping out of the machine. We feel a bond of compassion as we see through another's eyes and read their words. Books help us realize that everyone shares feelings of sorrow, joy, embarrassment, confusion, and loneliness.

We read books about other times and other places, but we can also read books by authors who actually lived long ago. The Grimm brothers wrote down the stories villagers told them in Germany nearly 200 years ago. Aesop was a legendary slave who lived in Samos in the sixth century B.C. Fables attributed to him were preserved through translations by Phaedrus and La Fontaine. Myths and legends from the Egyptian civilization are even older. We don't have DVDs or videotapes of these people or the way they lived. But we do have their words and, through books, they can still speak to us now.

Many of the advantages of reading alone don't have to wait until children actually learn how to read by themselves. Toddlers spend endless amounts of time looking at picture books, chewing on board books with lively illustrations, and carrying cloth books to bed with them. They also like to take waterproof books into the bathtub. Preschoolers play with pop-up books until they wear them out or tear them up into pieces. They can read most picture books from the pictures alone. All children can read wordless books — in any language!

Vivian was preparing dinner when her four-year-old son, Chris, asked, "Mommy, can you read me a book?" When Vivian told him to wait, Chris volunteered to go get the book. Chris left but did not come back.

Vivian explains, "It was very quiet and I wondered what he was doing. So I went to his room to check. There he was, sitting on the floor with the dog next to him. He had a book on his lap and he was reading to the dog! He asked the dog questions and then he gave the answer. He showed the pictures to the dog and slid his finger under the words just like I do. I couldn't believe that he was going through the exact same motions I use when we read together."

As a child learns to read on his own, he also discovers the benefits of reading aloud to others. He gets practice and develops confidence in himself by reading to his parents and to his younger brothers and sisters. Following the model you have given him, he begins to see himself as a reader; he is doing what readers do. He develops expressiveness in his reading, and his growing independence in reading alone is strengthened by the praise he receives from his listeners. He also, in turn, becomes another model for his younger siblings.

As children grow, the types of books that appeal to them change. Board books are popular with infants and toddlers. Three- and four-year-olds like big pictures and few words. Five- and six-year-olds learning to read like to reread alphabet books and counting books. Beginning readers pore over easy-to-read books until they can master them. When they move beyond the easy-to-read books, children want chapter books in which they can read one episode or one brief chapter without tiring. They explore riddle and joke books to discover short funny pieces they can tell to their friends. They love the music, rhyme, repetition, and wit of poetry. Many readers move to books in a series in which the same character meets one obstacle after another. Boys often move to science fiction while girls frequently prefer realistic novels. Whatever their tastes, there are books to please all readers. Our job is to find the best books to establish the reading habit. The reading habit, a seed planted early, takes deep root. You can nourish the seedling once it starts to grow, but the most important step is to get it planted.

Chapter 3: Getting Started

You may be like my adult daughter, Janie, who doesn't have a minute to call her own, and say you don't have time to add one more thing to your life. But you just did; you are reading this book! If you focus on raising readers, you'll have more free time in the future while your children are happily absorbed in a book on their own. There are some things you're already doing to instill the reading habit, so let's capitalize on them. You have the desire to make your children readers — that's the most important part.

You don't need to read this entire book right now. If your child is seven or eight years old, you may want to turn to the chapter on seven- and eight-year-olds. You'll find suggestions there about books to share and ways to share them. There are tips for busy parents that give you, at a glance, good ideas to put into immediate practice. Even if you have unlimited time, you might not want to do everything suggested here. Flip through this book until you spot one good idea and begin with that. No matter what age your child is, the time to start is now. Here are some suggestions for kids of all ages.

Ideas for Getting Started

1. *Keep books handy.* A stack of old favorites in a basket beside a big easy chair makes them convenient to grab at those moments a new activity is needed. Books on the bedside table show that reading is a natural part of the bedtime routine. A home library need not be expensive. With the low cost of paperbacks, you can have several for less than you pay for one breakable toy. Library cards are free. Trips to the library are a shared adventure and can bring in a new supply each week.

2. *Choose good books your child will like.* You will pay no more money for a really good book that your child will want to reread time and time again than you will pay for an uninteresting book that doesn't hold your child's attention. The lists at the back of this book offer suggestions for titles that have proven themselves popular with children, parents, and teachers. Use your trips to the library as the time to try out books. Buy a copy of the book your child wants repeatedly.

3. *Set a special time for reading.* I always read to my children at bedtime, but there was one other time that worked well, too. It was that fussy time just before dinner when we were waiting for Dad to come home. I distracted them with a book. I would get all three of them on my lap, one on each leg and one in the middle, and prop a big picture book right in front of us all. It soothed restless children and changed fussy time into happy time. Pick a time that works for you; even better would be three or four times a day! I know one mother who reads to her child at breakfast; it works if you are awake enough to see the page.

4. *Read at bedtime.* Reading at bedtime works wonders. When children are overly tired and bouncing off the wall, read them a story. Start with a short poem or two. The magic of the words and the sound of your soothing voice calms down even the most energetic kid. A comforting story might even head off a nightmare and ensure a restful sleep.

5. *Don't panic if you miss a day.* There are always interruptions to schedules in a busy family. Just pick up again when the interruption is past. It takes time to get into a new routine. Good habits are worth working for, and anything of lasting value takes work. In this case, however, the work is wrapped in pleasure and has longterm payoffs. Once you establish book time on a regular schedule, your child won't let you forget it.

6. *Read twenty minutes a day.* Of course, thirty minutes is even better. Allow enough time to finish a story or chapter and to talk about it. Use poetry to begin and end a story time.

7. *Talk about the story as you read.* If the story is set in the city, talk about how the pictures of buildings in the book look like buildings in your town. If there is a grandpa in the story, mention how he is or is not like his grandfather. If there are things your child doesn't understand, explain as you read. Listen to your child's comments and insights. Let her know that her thoughts are valuable. The talk surrounding a book is important, too.

8. *Mention the author and illustrator.* Discuss what these people do. Help the child to understand that somebody starts with a blank page and makes up a story. Look for favorite authors and illustrators. Discuss how their styles are consistent or how they change from book to book.

9. *Get others in on the reading act.* Make sure your partner takes a turn at reading. If you are a single parent, ask the baby-sitter or child-care provider to read as part of each day. Big brothers and sisters join in by reading to younger ones while you are busy folding clothes or fixing dinner. Grandparents, aunts, and uncles make good readers, too. This list of favorite things about grandparents appeared in a local newspaper:

GRANDMA	GRANDPA
Bakes cookies	Takes me fishing
Brings gifts	Loves sports TV
Hugs and kisses	Has a great lap
Never rushes me	Never agrees with Grandma
Reads to me	Tells me stories

Your child needs to see that everybody gets pleasure from reading. Your child also discovers that, though the words are the same, everybody reads the story differently. He sees that reading allows for individuality and creativity.

10. *Share your reactions to books you are reading.* If you are reading a good novel, tell your child how much you're enjoying it: "I just can't wait to see what happens," or, "This is such a good book. I just learned that whales sing songs to each other, hundreds of miles away in the ocean." Paraphrase a particularly good passage from your book for your child: "In my book, the writer says a tree is like a fountain of leaves. I've never thought of it that way before." A colleague of mine still recalls his fourth-grade class, where the teacher read aloud for a half hour each morning. One day, she was reading from *Uncle Tom's Cabin* and she became so absorbed in the story, she read well beyond the allotted time. She was in the midst of reading a particularly upsetting passage when she suddenly began crying. My friend remembers this as his first glimpse of how powerful reading can be; he respected books more from that moment on.

11. *If you can't answer your child's question, look up the answer in a book.* Consult a book with your child. Make it a positive activity, a treasure hunt for information.

Chapter 4: Reading on the Run

The care and feeding of readers doesn't have to be an overwhelming task. All you need is a little creativity to take advantage of opportunities to put books in front of your children. Kids have busy schedules, too, so make books available wherever they are. If they see you chuckling over a new book, they'll want to know what it's about.

This chapter is divided into four sections: (1) general activities for every day, (2) activities related to television viewing, (3) activities using computers, and (4) activities for special days and times.

General Activities for Every Day

If you have ever gone on a diet and starved yourself for a period of time, you lost weight. But as soon as you returned to your regular eating pattern, you went right back up to the weight you were. The same is true for books in the home: If you make books central to your life for two weeks and then forget about them, your children will fall into old ways. If you try to do just one thing — and do it regularly — it will work. The ideas here can be incorporated into your daily schedule without a lot of bother; they are ones you can keep on using. They have worked for other families and they'll work for you, too.

1. *Put books in places your child will be.* Availability is the name of the game. If books are beside the toy box, train set, dollhouse, or pet cage, they are more likely to be picked up. Keep books in the car or van. Put a tree house mystery book in a real or pretend tree house. Put children's cookbooks in the kitchen. Keep bedtime stories and poetry books beside the bed.

2. *Carry books for waiting rooms.* When you go to the dentist,

the doctor's office, the health clinic, or other places you may have to wait, have a book handy. Reading a story or a poem is a magical way to soothe a fretful child. Reading a poem from *Sing a Song of Popcorn* (Scholastic, 1988), a collection of verse compiled by Beatrice Schenk de Regniers, helps time to pass more quickly.

3. *Put books beside the bathtub.* My son-in-law is a bathtub soaker-reader, and my grandson has imitated his model. My grandson has already outgrown the waterproof-bathtub-book stage, so now his mother keeps paperbacks stacked beside the tub. In case one gets a little damp, it's easy to dry it out. Soaking in the tub with a good book is a positive habit to develop.

4. *Keep books in your child's room.* When children are "grounded" or sent to their room for "time-out," they need to find interesting things to do there. When they spend time in their room, they are free to read. They will choose reading more often if books are available. See the book lists at the end of this book for suggestions.

5. *Subscribe to magazines for your child.* Do you look forward to magazines arriving in your mailbox? Magazine subscriptions in your child's name will delight him and provide a new supply of reading material each month. There are more than 150 magazines for children. Look for *Highlights for Children, Cricket, Ranger Rick, Sesame Street, Time for Kids, Nickelodeon,* and *National Geographic World* for general interest columns, good stories, poems, word play, or articles about nature.

Everybody is busy, especially people with children. But there are little windows of time when you can get your child to read alongside other activities.

6. *Have your child help with the grocery list.* Make out your list of needed items and assign part of the list to your child.

One day I ran into Margot, a former student from New York University, standing near the checkout counter at the grocery store. As we chatted, her two children brought grocery items to put into her cart. Each time they delivered a product, she would show them the next item on the list and they would hurry off to find it. I congratulated her on teaching her children to read and she said, "Oh, they are saving me lots of steps, too."

7. *Read recipes.* All reading doesn't happen in books. When you're cooking something special, ask your child to read the ingredients or directions to you. Many books have recipes in them.

8. *Read road signs.* While you're driving, ask your child to read the STOP signs, YIELD signs, and other street signs.

9. *Carry books for traveling.* I never get on a subway, train, plane, or bus without a book. When you start out the door with the children, grab a book. It will make the journey more pleasant.

10. *Get taped recordings of books.* Many books have an audiocassette or CD available at libraries or for sale. Authors or professional performers read the books in a dramatic way. Most of us don't have time to read as much as we would like, but that is no reason our children should be denied this pleasure. If you don't have time to read to your child, let someone else do it.

11. *Make your own recordings.* If you have a tape recorder, record your own voice reading your child's favorite stories. If you're at work, your child can still be comforted by your voice. I have a friend whose son, Jeremy, was born prematurely. He was isolated from his mother for periods of time during the first few difficult weeks, so she made sure that tape recordings of her talking, reading, and singing lullabies were played near him to soothe him during those separations.

Activities Related to Television

First, realize that a television set doesn't have to be a monster lurking in your living room. Nor does it have to be your child's constant companion and babysitter. How this machine affects your family depends on how you use it. You can use your stove to cook nutritious meals or to fry junk food. But you don't blame the stove if you gain weight or have a stomachache.

Television can be fun to watch. It's colorful, easy, and distracting, and it's not surprising that your child might be drawn to that. You won't discourage your child from wanting to watch TV by simply saying it's bad for him, any more than you can discourage him from wanting to eat cookies. Make sure that television assumes its proper place in a challenging, diverse household. A child will watch TV out of boredom if there's nothing else to do; some children watch it more than thirty hours a week. As a parent, you can provide plenty of attractive alternatives. If you want reading to be one of those alternatives, make the effort to provide the books and to make reading appealing.

When your child does watch TV, consciously choose some shows that you will view with him. Look at a program guide and actively choose the shows together. In some households, the TV is always on, a distraction from other activities but not compelling enough to engage anyone's focus.

There are some good programs on television; look for them. If you subscribe to cable or satellite television, you have access to interesting educational documentaries on history, nature, biographies, and travel.

Television and books can complement each other by providing different perspectives on the same topic. Your child can learn a lot by reading about gorillas in a book, but he can learn something additional by watching them on a nature documentary. He can see how the gorillas move, how they carry their babies, how ferocious they look when provoked, what they sound like when they communicate. This is valuable, too.

The hard truth is, if you want your child to develop a healthy attitude toward television, you may have to reconsider your own viewing habits. As mentioned before, you are your child's most consistent and visible role model.

How can a family use television wisely?

1. *Watch TV shows that are related to books.* Many television programs encourage reading. When your child watches *Reading Rainbow, Arthur*, or *Between the Lions*, get the book featured on the show from a bookstore or library. Children willingly read stories they have seen on TV. Shows like *Blue's Clues* and *Sesame Street* have educational value that leads to extended reading.

2. *Make connections between TV shows and books.* If you see a news program about birds caught in an oil spill, get books from the library on endangered species, caring for the environment, or cleaning up oil spills.

3. *Limit the amount of television.* If you say, for example, "You may watch two programs each evening," your child needs to read the TV schedule to make critical judgments about which two programs to watch.

4. *Know what TV programs your child watches.* You know what books are in your child's library; be aware of what television shows she watches. Preview a new series to decide if it's appropriate for your child.

5. *Talk with your child about television stories.* Children have questions about what they see on TV; you need to discuss their misconceptions and questions. Good family shows cover important issues. Use a TV episode as a beginning point

for a family discussion. It might be that an episode is just like or just the opposite of what happens in your family. Talking with children about what they see helps clarify the difference between real life and televised stories.

6. *Talk about television writing.* Remind your child that, like books, television shows are written by somebody. How is the writing different? How important is the writing to the show?

7. *Share your own favorite programs.* If you are convinced that television shows were better in the past, you're in luck. So many channels carry reruns of old series, you can probably find *Little House on the Prairie*, *The Cosby Show*, *Full House*, *Bewitched*, or *The Brady Bunch*.

8. *Use a DVD player or VCR.* If you own a DVD player or a videocassette recorder, your family can gain considerable control over television viewing. As with books, children enjoy watching favorite videotapes and DVDs again and again, and you know what they're watching. *Tuck Everlasting*, *Charlotte's Web*, and *Because of Winn-Dixie* are a few of the many good books that have been made into movies. You can rent them from a video store or borrow them from a library. Television programs can be recorded and watched at designated "TV times" or at times that don't interfere with dinner, a family game, or conversation. If Aunt Betsy drops by for a visit, she doesn't have to compete with a television show in progress. A recorded show can be stopped and shown later.

9. *Don't allow your child to control the TV.* You don't allow your child to turn on the stove or the dishwasher or the car. Make it clear to your young child that turning on the television is also for grown-ups only.

10. *Think twice before buying a TV for your child's room.* If you think it's important to know what your child is watching on television and how often he watches it, you might want to

maintain the shared, community aspect of watching television by restricting all viewing to a family room.

11. *Find a quiet place for you and your child to read.* Try to provide a quiet place in the house for reading, but if that's not possible and the television set is on when you want to read, you can ignore it when you're absorbed in a good book. Children like snug, cozy places. Use pillows to create a cozy spot behind the sofa, near a bed, or under the stairs. Even if you need to be in the same room with the television set, you can create a special place for reading.

Computers, E-mail, Web sites

Like television, the personal computer is becoming a staple of many households. And like television, it can be an addictive medium, luring impressionable children to spend hours playing games, e-mailing friends, and surfing the Web. Time spent on computers can be wasteful, or it can be a genuinely valuable way to learn and to explore. There are numerous software programs that offer exercises for children learning to read. Several popular programs, featuring such literary characters as Clifford, Winnie-the-Pooh, and Arthur, offer activities to build word recognition, spelling, and vocabulary. Some invite children to scurry through scavenger hunts and solve multistep problems in order to answer riddles. A Magic School Bus program whisks kids away to explore the rain forest. There are interactive story books and programs for making greeting cards and banners.

The Internet provides online access to many children's magazines. A child can read current and back issues of *Time for Kids* (www.pathfinder.com/TFK/), *National Geographic World* (www.nationalgeographic.com), and other popular magazines. Many publishers of children's books, such as

Random House and Scholastic, have their own Web sites. Some offer interviews with authors, where children can participate by submitting their own questions. Some authors and illustrators, such as Jan Brett and Dav Pilkey, have their own Web sites, too. There is an Internet Public Library Youth Division (www.ipl.org/youth) and a Children's Literature Web Guide (www.acs.ucalgary.ca/~dkbrown/index.html). Certain book series have their own specific sites. Online booksellers can track down and sell you hard-to-find books from all over the world.

All this being said, it's hard for me to imagine that a computer could ever replace a book. There's something so special about feeling a book in your own hands, carrying it in your pocket, making notes in the margin, passing it on to a friend. Home computers can provide a family with information about children's literature and can provide children with readily available, quality reading material to supplement the books and magazines in the home. Many children are learning to use computers at younger ages. It will be interesting to see the long-term effects on the writing and reading skills of the first computer-literate generation.

Activities for Special Days and Times

Life should not be all work and no play. There are weekends, summer vacations, school breaks, birthdays, holidays, rainy days, and snowy days. There are times that books make a difference. They are also days that provide a little more free time. There are times that books fill in long hours when a child is sick or in the hospital. Books are just right for happy times and sad ones.

1. *Buy a birthday book.* When a child receives a book for his birthday, he recognizes that books are special gifts. If possible,

send a book to your school library to celebrate your child's birthday. Some schools have bookplates to inscribe the name of the child who is honored by the book gift.

2. *Make a rainy-day book.* Staple a few sheets of paper together to create a book with your child as the illustrator. Write down the sounds of rain — *ping, splash, patter.* Use these sounds to write a poem. Draw pictures of rain equipment — boots, raincoats, umbrellas. Recent fun books about the rain include *Rain* by Robert Kalan, *The Umbrella* by Jan Brett, *Have You Seen My Duckling?* by Nancy Tafuri, *Who Is Tapping at My Window?* by A. G. Deming, *Mushroom in the Rain* by Mirra Ginsburg, and *In the Rain with Baby Duck* by Amy Hest. Seeing what others do to celebrate the rain gives your children models for their own books.

3. *Read on snowy days.* When it's snowing, it's a good time to snuggle down cozily with a book. Try Ezra Jack Keats's *The Snowy Day*, in which Peter plays in the snow all day long. Peter hits a snow-covered branch and tries to save a snowball for another day by putting it in his pocket. Do some of the things Peter does in his story — make snow angels, hit snow-covered branches, build a snowman. Write out a recipe for snow ice cream and let your child follow the directions.

4. *Read before vacations.* When you are getting ready for a vacation, get some books from the library or travel agency. Read about the place you are going. Don't limit your reading to travel brochures. There are excellent informational books about national parks, historical sites, and resort areas. There are also fictional stories set in all parts of the country and world. Ask your children's librarian to point out books set in the area you will be visiting.

If the books are too difficult for your child to manage reading alone, vary the pattern by reading them aloud. Your child learns that reading is a source of information for all endeavors.

5. *Read during vacations.* If you travel, books are a vital part of your luggage. Take books along. Encourage your child to keep a journal or diary. Write a book together about places you see.

6. *Read after vacations.* Traveling to new places brings up as many questions as it answers. Take notes on topics you and your child want to explore further when you return home. If your family had a picnic by an old lighthouse, find a book about a lighthouse. If your child met his first camel at the zoo, read a book about a camel. You will be reinforcing your child's realization of the connection between books and his own life.

7. *Read at home.* If you stay at home, books are an even more important part of vacation time. Set a quiet reading time each day. Vacations at home are the time to tackle thick books that take a week or so to read. They're also a good time to demonstrate to your child how far you can travel in a book even if you don't leave the house. During the many weeks of summer vacation, it is particularly important that your child continues to read. Research shows that by September, some students who do not read during the summer score much lower on reading tests than they did in the spring.

8. *Read holiday books. The Night Before Christmas* by Clement C. Moore is always a favorite. A recent edition published by Putnam has delightful illustrations by Jan Brett. *Lyle at Christmas* by Bernard Waber follows the holiday antics of Lyle the Crocodile. Another release is *Beni's First Hanukkah* by Jane Breskin Zalben. Diane Hoyt-Goldsmith's *Celebrate Kwanzaa* suggests ideas for the holiday. The text describes the observance of the seven Kwanzaa principles and gives a quotation for each day.

9. *Make a holiday book.* For each holiday, make a book with your child showing your family traditions. Include a section on

special foods, house decorations, family rituals, and activities. Add pictures and write poems. You are not only involving your child in reading and writing but you are passing along your family heritage.

Did You Know . . .

- Kids who are read to do better in school.
- The context in which reading occurs influences what will be remembered.
- Children of talkative mothers perform better than do children of quiet mothers; they use a larger vocabulary, they show more curiosity, and they display a more vivid and active imagination.
- Infants can distinguish their mothers' voices from others very early in life.
- Everyday experiences contribute to a child's mental development.
- A child's brain is active from the beginning. The way we talk to a child makes a difference in learning.
- Reading aloud to a child raises self-esteem and reading ability.
- Becoming a better reader helps a child to do better in all subjects.
- Research shows that more than eleven hours of television a week is related to a drop in a child's scholastic achievement.
- Keeping a diary helps a child become a better writer and reader.
- Reading the print on cereal boxes is good practice for a child.
- More than 90 percent of all information that comes to our brain is visual.

- Allowing your child to read in bed is a good habit to encourage.
- Children will read a book on their own that has been read aloud to them.
- When children hear book language, it helps them understand more complex language.

Chapter 5: Infants, Toddlers, and Preschoolers

Life with Infants, Toddlers, and Preschoolers

Infants:
- Like action nursery rhymes
- Imitate actions of children in books
- Make sounds of animals in books
- Relate books to real life
- Like to see babies in books
- Pick favorite books from the shelf
- Enjoy the three R's: rhythm, repetition, and rhyme
- Listen to nursery rhymes and Mother Goose verses as they are rocked
- Fall asleep to nursery songs and lullabies

> In the great green room
> There was a telephone
> And a red balloon
> And a picture of —
> The cow jumping over the moon.

I know the book *Goodnight Moon* by heart. I read it countless times to my youngest grandchild, Trisha, when she was an infant. I'm always grateful to have another chance to read all the old favorites. Trisha heard those favorites read by her mother, father, brother, sister, visiting grandparents, aunts, and uncles. She has been bathed in books since she was born. At sixteen months of age, Trisha would sit for forty-five minutes while someone read to her and talked with her about the pictures in a book.

If you read a book to Trisha with animals in it, she would

say, "Grr, meow, quack quack, moo" and point to the pictures of the animals. She imitated the children in books; when they clapped their hands, she clapped hers. When they jumped up and down, Trisha jumped up and down. If the child in a book took a bath, Trisha would leap up out of my lap and try to pull off her shirt and socks as she ran toward the tub shouting "Bubble! Bubble!" Some people say we need to "catch 'em in the cradle" to make children readers, but with Trisha we had to catch her on the run.

Trisha loved to look at pictures of babies in books. She never tired of patting the picture and saying "baby, baby!" seemingly fascinated with someone who looked like her. She carried books around with her, clutching them to her chest the same way she carried her teddy bear. Trisha said, "Book, book," and went to the shelf to get one as a means of asking someone to read to her.

Trisha had a perfect record with pop-up books; she demolished every one read to her. She would grab the picture that flipped up and hand it to her mother to show her the pretty picture. She was fascinated by the movement and, quicker than you could grab her hand, she had grabbed the page. So much for another pop-up book. We glued, taped, and stapled pieces to try to rescue Trisha-ized books. Trisha is a teenager now — an avid reader who knows how to handle pop-up books!

As a grandmother, I know why we must read to our children, but as a young mother I did not realize its importance. I had been a kindergarten teacher for a few years and knew the place of books in a classroom, but I didn't understand the critical need to have books at home. Our children loved stories; when my father came to visit, he told our children the same stories he had told me as a child. They begged for more just as I had done. Grandpa's stories were most often about tracking wild animals, and as the children got bigger so did the size of the wild animals he hunted. A wonderful storyteller, Grandpa matched the length of each scary chase through the woods to fit the length of their attention span. Today, I do more book reading than storytelling to my grandchildren; perhaps I depend too much on other people's stories instead of my own. Children need both.

Toddlers:
- Like to read the same books over and over
- Look at board books
- Choose a particular book among many
- Repeat Mother Goose verses by heart
- Explore the world by tasting, climbing, touching it
- Like short rhyming stories
- Like large, clear, realistic pictures
- Like to name objects in books and magazines
- Like bathtub books and toy books

Emilia is two and a half years old and is obsessed with Peter Rabbit. She goes to the library with one of her parents several times a month, and on a recent trip she checked out a series of Beatrix Potter classics that happened to fit her little hands perfectly. After three or four readings, Dan, her father, was no longer allowed to read them to her. "My books, Daddy," she would say, pulling them away. Now when you ask her her name, she'll say, "Peter Rabbit." She calls Dan "Daddy Rabbit," and her mother, Alison, is now officially "Mommy Rabbit." Emilia would never touch vegetables before, but now she begs for carrots. When she had a tummyache, she asked her father for the prescription recommended in the book—parsley—which she holds in her hand. She has also requested numerous cups of "cammy me" (chamomile tea), because that's what Peter's mother gave him. Emilia no longer likes cats, because Peter didn't. And when she goes to sleep, it's in her "Sand Bank."

Books can make a big impression on children at this age. Lucy had been surrounded by books since birth. Aunt Maura invited Lucy over to spend the night. Her mother said it was okay, so Lucy ran to her room to pack her suitcase. When her mother checked the suitcase, she found seven books in it, nothing else. She said to Lucy, "Where are your clothes?" Lucy replied, "Oh, I forgot."

Preschoolers:
- Use words to express themselves
- Struggle for independence: "Wanna do it myself"
- Play with language, sing-song, nonsense sounds
- Know nursery rhymes
- Are fascinated by other children, share grudgingly
- May create an imaginary friend
- Are fearful of the dark and strangers
- Like simple folktales but not fairy tales

When Luis was four years old, he was chock-full of energy. He charged in the door from nursery school ready to eat, play, watch TV, and pester his mother all at the same time. His older sister, Marta, was a calming influence on him, but Marta was most often at school or out with her friends.

One day, Marta was teaching Luis a new song, "The Eensy Weensy Spider." She sang it a couple of times using the hand motions, and Luis joined her on the second round. The action was a bit too complicated for Luis's four-year-old coordination; he wiggled all his fingers as he mimicked the spider crawling up the waterspout.

Marta decided to give Luis another way to interpret the spider and the waterspout song. She gave him a marker and a big piece of paper. Luis happily scribbled on the paper, making large circular movements as he sang about the spider crawling up the waterspout. He brought his marker down hard across the page with a *whoosh* when the rain comes down, then started spiraling the spider marks back up the page again. The finished product looked mostly like big round scribbles, but Marta decided that it was good enough to tape on the refrigerator door. Marta said, "Now that we are here at the refrigerator, maybe it's time for a little juice and crackers." After Luis settled down, Marta pulled out a new pop-up book she had brought home for Luis about the eensy weensy spider. Luis handled it tenderly because it was a special gift from a special person in his life. He read it like an angel, gently pulling out the tabs to make the spider move.

Making a Reader out of Your Preschooler

You have all the preschool years to send an important message to your child: Reading is fun! There need be little stress on learning word and letter sounds. Emphasize the fun.

Of course, talk about the story and the characters. Ask, "What do you think is going to happen next?" Answer questions, too — any that your child asks. But don't ask questions the way a teacher asks questions. Ponder out loud, "Mmmm, wonder what he's going to do now?" Your questions don't require precise answers; they keep the child's interest focused on the story.

When you pick up a new book, you might say, "I wonder what this story is going to be about?" This question introduces and underscores a very important message — that a story is *about* something. You are indicating that a story has meaning and that we discover the meaning by reading the words.

That's the real reason for reading. You are laying the basic groundwork for a lasting understanding. Reading is getting meaning. You may wonder why I'm making such an issue of this simple concept. It's because I've seen children say the words on a page perfectly and yet when I ask them, "What did you just read?" they say, "I don't know."

This is the difference between simply pronouncing the sounds of words and really reading (getting meaning). Saying words is not reading. Children who settle for just pronouncing sounds become the students who have problems reading in school—they don't expect reading to make sense! Good readers expect things to make sense; they settle for nothing less.

This is not to say that books need to be serious to have meaning. Even silly poems and jingles tell a story, and you and your child can have great fun reading them. When you read Dr. Seuss's *On Beyond Zebra*, you giggle at the make-believe words and animals. When you say jingly Mother Goose rhymes, you laugh at the wordplay and say the delicious sounds over and over. Again, children take their cues from the way you react to the story; you are their model.

When you read to your preschooler, invite her to join in on the repetitive phrases — she'll probably do it automatically. Preschoolers also like to fill in the gaps when you read together. Start this with Mother Goose or other rhyming lines and continue the practice with nonrhyming texts. Read "Humpty Dumpty sat on a —. Humpty Dumpty had a great —." Children know which word to insert because it rhymes or makes sense; this gives them confidence that they know what words will come next. The ability to anticipate is an important skill in reading.

If the print for a word is in larger type, read it louder; if it's wiggly or wavy, read it in a wavering voice; if it's tiny, read it softly. You're showing your child that we get clues from print. Ask your child to say words from print along with you; it is a beginning step — just the way she held onto your finger as she took those first wobbly steps in walking.

Everything you do when you read to your preschooler is paving the way for him to read alone. When a kindergarten teacher opens a book to read to five-year-olds, *your* child will know what to expect and how to participate. He'll know how to hold a book, how to turn pages, and how to enjoy the experience because he heard stories at home. You are making a reader out of your child.

Making a Writer out of Your Preschooler

The connections between early reading and early writing are still being explored, but we already know some things for sure. We know that there are certain developmental stages all children seem to go through. Children gradually discover aspects of writing that we take for granted, such as capital letters, periods, and words going from left to right across a page. Children discover them in a somewhat similar order. They gradually discover that writing (at least in English) goes from left to right. They learn that we keep the letters on a straight line going across a page. They learn that words are represented by letters, that words are separated by a space, and that reading requires looking at the words instead of the pictures.

In the early years, children do not distinguish between writing and drawing. If you ask children entering kindergarten if they know how to read, 90 percent will say no. But when you ask the same children if they know how to write, most will say yes. One day in a kindergarten class, I asked Billy what he was going to write about. He said, "How do I know? I haven't even drawed it yet." Children seem to draw first and write later. We help them if we write down what they say about their pictures.

Research shows that writing ability often develops prior to reading ability. When a child writes, he pays attention to print and learns that letters represent sounds. That knowledge opens the door to reading.

In learning to write, children move from primitive drawing skills to the ability to form the letter "O" or to make circles. Individual experiences differ greatly, but there are general developmental patterns in writing you might observe. Their early attempts will be scribbles, but eventually they make recognizable objects and letters. It's the same way in speaking. Children first call all men "Daddy" but then narrow that term down to the one person who is their father. They call all four-legged animals "horsey" until they refine the categories and call some doggies, cows, or zebras.

Writing development depends heavily upon eye-hand motor coordination, as well as visual discrimination. Children can distinguish between letter forms before they are actually able to write them. In this, as in all learning, let the child be the guide. Don't insist that he make the letters the way you do; he'll come to that gradually. When you think about the letters of the alphabet as fifty-plus geometric forms, you realize how much your child needs to remember. The uppercase letters don't look a whole lot like lowercase letters — and yet we call them the same thing. Adults learning the Greek alphabet are just as perplexed as children learning English, and yet adults already know the alphabetic principle — that words are represented by letters that proceed across a page and are separated by spaces.

The first word your child will write is probably her own name. Stick with uppercase (capital) letters so that she sees it the same way for a while. A child will insist that "Cindy" is not her name; her name is "CINDY." Kindergarten teachers are happy if children come to school knowing how to write their first names.

For now, put her name on the refrigerator with magnetic letters. Put it on her books. A child's name holds immense fascination. After learning her name, the second message a child writes is often, "I luv u." What parent can resist that message?

Tips for Busy Parents

During the preschool years, your child is a learning machine — he learns even when you don't know he's learning. The most important things you want your child to do are:

- To love books and stories
- To learn about language
- To learn to handle books

You can accomplish these worthwhile learning tasks if you do some simple things.

1. *Read a bedtime story.* This ritual cannot be established too

early or repeated too often. The quiet, private times when you and your child are close together are essential to establishing a lifelong habit.

2. *Read the same books over and over.* You may get bored like the father who said, "If I have to read *Goodnight Moon* one more time, I think I'll die." First of all, be assured that one more reading probably won't kill you. You may have said the same thing about changing diapers, but you survived that, too. For your child, hearing a favorite story again is the repetition of a happy experience, one he wants again and again.

We all value rituals in our lives, whether it's the morning coffee with a newspaper or a hot bath at night. For a child, the ritual reading of the same comforting story can signal that it's bedtime and can actually help him to fall asleep. For your sake, after enough readings you can recite the story from memory to entertain or soothe your child even if you don't have the book with you. Ask your child to say the story with you.

3. *Give your child nontoxic markers, pens, or pencils and plenty of paper.* Children need to make marks on paper to learn that what we say can be written down, and that they can write, too. I recently watched a father and daughter on a train sharing an artist's huge sketch pad. She was happily entertained drawing hats and as she showed her father her artwork, her father made interested comments such as, "I like this hat so much I would wear it to work. You'd better write the name of that hat beside it so I can show the name to the people in the hat store." And, using many of her own unique letters, she wrote "daddy hat." I know you don't like marks on your walls or furniture any more than I do, but don't deny your child this crucial learning experience of writing. Keep writing supplies in a special place to bring out while you are busy but can keep an eye on the writer. The masterpieces your child

creates can then be displayed on your refrigerator or dated and kept in a folder.

4. *Write messages to your child.* When you need to be away, leave a message to be read to your child. Isaac's mother put a little poem or message in his lunch box every day.

5. *Write down your child's spoken words.* Let your child see that his words are important. Read the words back to the child. Give the writing to someone else to read; show that others can read the words, too. Your child can tell you a funny story or a wish for today. Write a poem about it. Together, you can write about your child's drawings.

6. *Label your child's possessions.* Name tags are not just for use when packing for camp. If clothes are to be handed down to the next child — something we all do — use just the last name or initials. Children need to see their names on everything.

7. *Label objects in the house.* Tara writes words like "stove," "door," and "table" on index cards and tapes them to the appropriate object so her two young daughters can clearly connect the spoken word, the written word, and the object.

8. *Get alphabet books and make alphabet books.* Visit your local library for some good alphabet books. Or make your own alphabet book. Staple together twenty-six pages of paper, then write a letter on each page. Your child fills each page with words or pictures that begin with that letter. She can cut the pictures from old magazines or draw them herself. She can write her name and the names of her friends on the appropriate pages. You can help when necessary.

9. *Put magnetic letters on the refrigerator.* Many children have learned to read from magnetic letters on the refrigerator. Of course, you need to form them into words, especially your child's name, and invite him to do the same. We put things on the refrigerator that we want people to notice. My friend Norman wrote a story for his granddaughter. When he called

to see if she had received and enjoyed it, he asked, "What did you do with it?" She answered, "I put it on the refrigerator!"

Did You Know . . .

- Infants can see color and shapes very early in life.
- Preschoolers like to hear the same story over and over again.
- A child still in the womb grows accustomed to her mother's voice.
- Preschoolers like to sing, chant, and tell stories.
- Listening is a receptive skill that requires preschoolers to think and interpret.
- Speaking and listening habits profoundly influence a preschooler's ability to write.
- Infants, toddlers, and preschoolers understand many more words than they can say.
- Preschoolers need to see that reading and writing are useful and enjoyable things to do.
- Preschoolers' natural curiosity and desire to make sense of their world are the only motivation they need to learn.
- Preschoolers learn by doing things—actively exploring books and print.

Chapter 6: Five- and Six-year-olds

Life with Five- and Six-year-olds

Five-year-olds:
- Like stories with animals that talk
- Like simple folktales and some fairy tales
- Like a prince and a princess
- Believe in magic and accept make-believe
- Think fairy-tale characters actually lived a long time ago
- Recognize some letters of the alphabet
- Can write their names

Five-year-old Emily and her three-year-old brother, Andrew, hear about six stories a day; both Mom and Dad read to them. The children connect the stories they hear to real life. When birds came up to the feeder last winter, Andrew went to find *A Year of Birds* by Ashley Wolff and pointed to the feeding station. When Andrew lost his teddy bear, Emily said he was just like the boy in John Burningham's book *The Blanket*, who had everybody in the house looking for it. Everyone looked for Andrew's bear the same way everybody had looked for the lost blanket; both were found under their owner's pillows.

Emily has her favorite stories; she has memorized Bill Martin, Jr.'s *Brown Bear, Brown Bear* and she loves to recite everything the Very Hungry Caterpillar ate on Saturday. She quietly hands another book to a guest for a third reading and whispers confidentially, "Andrew can't read yet!" Of course, Emily can't read yet, either, but, luckily, she doesn't know it.

Emily was an emergent reader, memorizing books, joining in on refrains, retelling stories to Andrew, and connecting them to her own life. Six months later, Emily was a reader. She had played at reading until she became a real reader.

Six-year-olds:
- Recognize the letters of the alphabet
- Can count to one hundred
- Can write about ten words from memory
- Are able to read easy-to-read books
- Still like fairy tales
- Like having someone read to them
- Memorize poetry and nonsense verse
- Enjoy alphabet and counting books
- Search for simple informational books
- Like books about dinosaurs
- Write words the way they sound

As I located seat 6C on the plane, I smiled to find a child and her mother as my seatmates. In a few minutes, I discovered that the winsome child was named Lauren, that she was six years old, in the first grade, and that she was on her way to serve as flower girl in her aunt's wedding. Before long, I pulled two books by Bill Martin, Jr., *Brown Bear, Brown Bear* and *Chicka Chicka Boom Boom*, out of my book bag and read them with Lauren. I read the first page, "Brown Bear, Brown Bear, what do you see? I see a Red Bird looking at me."

Lauren picked up the patterned language quickly and read the next page, "Red Bird, Red Bird, what do you see? I see a Yellow Duck looking at me." She also grasped the pattern of the other book, "A told B, and B told C, I'll meet you at the top of the coconut tree. Chicka chicka boom boom! Will there be enough room?"

Together we enjoyed the lilting rhythmic flow of Bill Martin's words as we sailed through the sky toward Minneapolis. It was easy for Lauren to chime in readily because she identified the strong pattern and knew what was coming next; she could predict the words because they rhymed. Like all beginning readers, Lauren read more fluently because the books had natural-sounding, rhythmic language. I told Lauren's mother how impressed I was with Lauren's ability to read.

Lauren was a beginning first grader, and yet she could read along with the rhythmic pattern of the language in the stories easily. Later during the flight, Lauren showed me the reading book she carried with her from school. It was stuffed with several worksheets assigned for Lauren to complete "so she wouldn't miss anything" while she was away on flower-girl duty. Lauren's book contained the following story:

Ann ran. Nan ran.
Ann and Nan ran and ran.
Ann ran to Nan.
Nan ran to Ann.

Lauren read this, too, but she read it more slowly and haltingly than she read the other stories. The short, stilted sentences caused her to read word by word.

Making a Reader out of Your Five- or Six-year-old

Five- and six-year-olds have a growing attention span; they are willing to stick with one task for nearly an hour if it interests them. This means we can read longer and more complex stories to them. Fives and sixes are on the verge of figuring out how to read for themselves; they ask endless questions, such as "What does that say?" Some children have already figured out how letters combine to make words and are striking out on their own as early readers. At this point, they are probably familiar with the meaning of language terms such as "word" and "sentence." Poetry is particularly helpful for these beginning readers as they discover the clever games authors play with words. These children need material that contains short, simple, and rhythmic language. Even precocious readers tire easily at this age when they are doing the reading; keep these reading sessions brief, happy, and successful.

Many children have access to communication devices from an early age. Some have direct access to a computer, television set, the Internet, or cellular telephones. I receive e-mail messages regularly from my grandchildren. Children are exposed to more visual and verbal interaction today than ever before in our history. They learn to manipulate visual and verbal symbols at early ages.

Five- and six-year-olds are developing a growing sense of independence, going off to school alone, dressing themselves, and caring for their personal needs. These signs bode well for intellectual development since the child can seek out information that interests her. Independence at this age, however, is like thin ice on a pond; it collapses easily if tested too heavily. Home and family provide the security that makes five- and six-year-olds brave and competent most of the time.

Many five- and six-year-old children are fearful: scared of the dark, strangers, and monsters. Their understanding of the line between real and make-believe is not firmly fixed. Five-year-old Yolanda startled her mother recently by asking point-blank, "Mommy, am I real?" The one-word answer is easy enough, but just try to explain away all the implications of a question like that. Children of this age don't like to take chances in case some of those monsters in books are real, too! They may want a certain book put away or taken out of their room before they can fall asleep. For example, Maurice Sendak's book *Where the Wild Things Are* has huge smiling monster wild things that are completely under the control of the little boy Max. The wild things don't want Max to leave their land, but he chooses to be where someone loves him best of all — home. When a child enjoys this book wrapped in the security of a parent's arms, there is nothing to fear. If your child feels differently about it, just put the book away for a while — he will relish it later.

Making a Writer out of Your Five- or Six-year-old

Five- and six-year-olds love to make marks on paper; they are far beyond the scribble stage and are making real letters and words. They use both pictures and letters, mixing them freely to put their meanings on paper. During this period, children are working on the relationships between letters and sounds. They try to figure these out by themselves, and many children succeed.

As children become writers, they invent spellings for words they want to use. Invented spelling is what we call temporary spelling before children learn all the rules adults use to spell. At this early stage, misspellings are not "wrong" any more than a child is wrong to lose balance or stumble when he's first learning to walk. Temporary, invented spelling is simply a step in the process of learning to write. In fact, children's temporary spellings give us a window on what they know. If a five- or six-year-old spells dinosaur "dnsr" we see that he is using beginning sounds heavily and is relying on the consonant sounds instead of vowels. This is exactly what he should be doing at his developmental stage.

Invented spelling does *not* interfere with children's ability to spell correctly later. It is an appropriate developmental step, just like the "mmmm" and "dddd" sounds your child made as a beginning speaker. There are lots of advantages for the child at this age who uses invented spelling.

Invented Spelling:
- Encourages children to make connections between sound and letters
- Helps children become independent as writers; they don't need to ask others how to spell words
- Encourages children to write longer, more colorful stories; they can write anything they can say. Writing more equals writing better.
- Helps children go beyond words they know how to read; they are not limited to writing only words they can read
- Encourages children to take responsibility for their own learning; they are in control of what they write and the way they write it; they make the writing system their own
- Provides extensive practice in phonics; children practice their sounds as they write — using letters to represent the sounds they hear in words

There is a sequence that almost all children follow in their invented-spelling development. Inventive spellers often use the names of the letters and not just the sounds we say the letters represent. For example, they may begin *elephant* with "L," spell you "U," and why "Y." They learn to use long vowels (ā as in cake) before short vowels (ă as in task) because they hear the sound of the letter name in the long vowels. Long vowels say their own names. Developmental stages in invented spelling hinge upon technical and complicated detail; at this stage you only need to encourage your child to use invented spelling and watch his control of it grow.

Here is a sample from Michael, a five-year-old, written on a computer:

My bruthr had the chicin pox.
dad told him that hee is
gowing to get a beec and litl wit
fethrs growing awt of his armpits.
and a litl red com wil grow awt of
the top of his hed. hee got scard.
I didn't get scard beecorz I noow hee
wuz onleey teesing.

This is another of Michael's stories demonstrating invented spelling:

This is a storey about me,
Wen I snees the holl worlld spins a
rouwnd wen I snees the flours blow
awa and wen I snees the gras jumps.
And wen I snees the holl room shacs.
And wen I snees evereey botey ses
Michael you are to louwd.

Parents are often concerned that their children will never learn how to spell correctly. Invented spelling is only a developmental step. Children will receive spelling instruction and see correctly spelled words in books they read. They become better writers earlier if they are free to use invented spellings; they can express themselves more freely.

Tips for Busy Parents

Joanne, a former reading teacher, has a son, Steve, who had difficulty learning to read in the first grade. Figuring out each word was so slow and painful that Steve never seemed to get any fun from reading. He couldn't concentrate on the meaning because he was struggling so hard to figure out the words. Joanne talked with Steve's teacher and they made a plan. Each day, Steve brought home a book from school and Joanne would read one page and Steve would read the next. They would cuddle up in a chair or Joanne would lie beside him on his bed and they would take turns reading. A few months later, Steve's teacher called Joanne and said, "Whatever you're doing is really working. Steve is just zooming along with reading. He has caught fire as a reader and is making terrific progress." The assisted reading that Joanne did with Steve seemed to be the key to fluent reading for him.

1. *You read to me and I'll read to you.* Beginning readers need help in moving from word-by-word reading to smooth, meaningful reading. Take turns reading with your child. You read one page and let the child read the next. John Ciardi's book of poetry, *You Read to Me, I'll Read to You*, is written for just this kind of exchange, with pages alternating between adult vocabulary and first-grade vocabulary. Read the same book several times. On repeated readings, let your child take over more of the reading.

2. *Fill in the blanks.* Reading poetry and verse that rhymes is a terrific way to lead your five- or six-year-old into reading. Read the phrases all the way through for part of the poem or verse. On repeated readings, stop before you reach the end of the next rhyming line and let your child provide the rhyming word.

3. *Play sounds games.* While you are preparing a meal, driving,

walking, or cleaning, play a game about sounds with your child. A simple starter is: "Riddle, riddle, ree. I see something you don't see. And it starts with T." Your child guesses what you see and takes the next turn. Start with the sounds at the beginnings of words; they are the ones children learn first. As your child becomes more adept, you can move to the sounds at the ends of words: ". . . and it ends with K."

4. *Make a calendar.* Use one sheet of paper for each month. Write the days of the week across the top and put in the numeral one for the first day of the month. Let your child finish the calendar, writing in special events coming up. Whether you do one month or an entire year depends on your child's maturity and your patience.

5. *Write a fill-in-the-blank story.* Make up a simple story frame or use a familiar folktale, such as "The Three Little Pigs." Write "Once upon a time there were _____. They told their _____ they were going out to seek their _____." Your child fills in the names of the characters and other important words. Praise the ones he gets right.

6. *Write a biography or autobiography.* Five- and six-year-old children like to write about themselves and can do so with your help. Use the same technique of writing in parts that are too difficult and allowing your child to fill in names and important words. For example, "_____ was born on _____. S/he weighed _____ pounds and _____ ounces. The first visitor was _____."

7. *Value your child's stories.* "That is such a funny story, you should write it down and send it to Uncle Jack, or your friend Lisa in Chicago, or tell it to your dad." If her stories are ignored, a child will think she has nothing of value to write about. Let her know that her life *is* worthy of writing about. Dramatize the story.

8. *Make sentence strips.* Write a sentence about your family.

Cut it into pieces and ask your child to put it together again.

9. *Make a board game.* Choose one of your child's favorite books as the basis for a board game. Use the events or episodes in the book to divide steps along a path the characters must travel. Use small objects to represent the characters. Make a spinner to determine how many steps each player can take. The object of the game can be to see who arrives first at the end of the story.

10. *Start a collection.* Create dividers in a small box to hold objects your child collects. A walk in the woods will yield acorns, nuts, leaves, small stones, bird feathers, and seed pods. A walk in your neighborhood may uncover pebbles, keys, coins, and who knows what. A walk along the beach leads to seashells and driftwood. A collection of objects related to a favorite book is also fun. Label the objects in the collection to use reading and writing skills.

11. *Cook from a book.* Prepare food inspired by a book. For example, *Chicken Soup with Rice*, *Green Eggs and Ham*, and *Stone Soup* are naturals. Some books include recipes for the character's favorite food. Look for books with easy recipes for children, such as *Pretend Soup and Other Real Recipes: A Cookbook for Preschoolers & Up* by Mollie Katzen and *Quick and Easy Cookbook* by Robyn Supraner.

Did You Know . . .

- Children who know how to handle books and are familiar with stories learn how to read more quickly than those who have little or no book experience.
- Children who learn to read early are the ones who are read to by parents, siblings, or other caregivers.
- The rhythmic sound of a mother's heart establishes the sta-

bility and comfort of a regular beat while a child is still in the womb — which may explain some of the appeal of poetry.

- Reading aloud to your child is the single most important thing you can do to make him a reader.
- A five-year-old child has a speaking vocabulary of approximately 2,000 words.
- Telling a story from the pictures is an important step in the learning-to-read process.
- When the brain makes connections between something new and something already known, it forms new lines, new connections. The more connections made, the more learning occurs.
- Pretending to read is a critical step in the developmental process of learning to read.
- Talking develops language. Talk with your child and get her to talk about things you do together and things she does with friends.
- Most children learn to work on a computer more quickly than their parents do. Computers facilitate reading and writing.

Chapter 7: Seven-and Eight-year-olds

Life with Seven-and Eight-year-olds

Seven-year-olds:
- Develop budding friendships
- Seek acceptance by other children their age
- Show increasing independence from home and family
- Strike out on their own as readers
- Take pride in showing off their reading skills
- Understand more complex stories than they can read
- See the world as good/bad; fair/not fair
- Believe in magic
- Accept fairy-tale "eye-for-an-eye" morality and cruel justice

A short poem Rachel wrote sums up this seven-year-old pretty well:

I like books.
I like pears.
I like dancing on the chairs.

Rachel loves her dance classes. She performed a hula number in one recital and was a fairy in a recent production of *Peter Pan*. She just learned to do cartwheels in class, so now she does them all over the house. She also enjoys swimming and in-line skating. Rachel likes to read chapter books from the American Girl series.

When her parents read aloud to her, Rachel often reads alternate pages with them. She reads with good inflection, but occasionally reads too fast. At this age, kids can get so excited about their new skills, quantity is sometimes more attractive than quality. When Rachel and her classmates started keeping journals in school, it became a contest to see who could write the most words for a while. When asked what she likes best about reading, Rachel says, "I like to learn new words." She just learned that *house* has a "u" in it and she thinks it's pretty funny that she's been writing about living in a *hose* for the past few weeks. She practiced some of her writing skills and expanded her vocabulary by using the Reader Rabbit and JumpStart programs on her family's personal computer.

As a young mother, I sometimes read a few picture books to my children that were left over from my teaching days, but I didn't make a point of taking my children to the library or building their home book collection. This began to change as firstborn Janie entered second grade. She wanted books she could try to read alone, so we went to the public library to find some. Janie, like many other children, led her parents into children's books.

When I finally took Janie to the library, we chanced upon Elsa Minarik's Little Bear books, which were illustrated by Maurice Sendak. Little did I realize that Janie was selecting books by the world's foremost illustrator. By looking at the world through a child's eyes, Janie and I discovered Ezra Jack Keats's *The Snowy Day*, Maurice Sendak's *Where the Wild Things Are*, and Marcia Brown's *Cinderella*. Janie continued to take me with her into exploring books of increasing complexity as she grew as a reader. While she was developing her wings as an independent reader, Janie discovered chapter books on the "C" shelf at the library; like a rabbit nibbling carrots, she read through the books of Beverly Cleary, Eleanor Clymer, Matt Christopher, Scott Corbett, Natalie Savage Carlson, Rebecca Caudill, Molly Cone, and Elizabeth Coatsworth.

One day, friend and mentor Charlotte Huck gave me a copy

of *Charlotte's Web* inscribed to "Bee and her family." I read this book aloud to the entire family. We laughed. We cried. We snuffled our way through at many points when I became choked up while reading about the friendship between a pig and a spider. This was the first truly significant children's novel I had ever read or my children had heard. It was a peak experience in our family. We began to look for more like it. We discovered A. A. Milne in *When We Were Very Young*, *Now We Are Six*, *Winne-the-Pooh*, and *The House at Pooh Corner*. We discovered Beatrix Potter's *The Tale of Peter Rabbit* and all her other animal books. We suppressed giggles and tears again through Kenneth Grahame's *The Wind in the Willows*. I remember sitting beside the children's bathtub to read the chapter "The Piper at the Gates of Dawn" and watching small tears slide down already wet faces. We puzzled our way through Lewis Carroll's *Alice's Adventures in Wonderland*.

Of course, we read other books, too, but these memorable ones became part of our lives. Even today we say, "He's a real Templeton" (the rat in *Charlotte's Web*) about a person who only does things for his own benefit; or, "He's a Toad" (like Toad in *The Wind in the Willows*) about a show-off. So many things happened during those years that were to last a lifetime. We forged bonds of love, we all became readers, and I, unknowingly, laid the foundation for my own career devoted to children's books.

Eight-year-olds:
- Reach peak of interest in fairy tales
- Begin interest in real-life stories
- Show beginning interest in sports
- Choose to read independently

- Like poetry/verse and chapter books
- Like riddles, jokes, off-the-wall humor
- Want to choose their own books

Years ago, I spent a week babysitting three of my grandchildren so their parents could take a much-needed rest. That week, eight-year-old Jason and I cleaned out his bookshelves. It was easy to pull out books Jason had outgrown—we just put them on another shelf to keep for his little sister, Trisha. It was more difficult to sift out the comic books he had collected. I wondered if he would ever read the comic books again, but Jason doesn't like to throw things away. We put all potential discards into a box and allowed him a last chance to rescue any treasures before the box went to the garage sale.

When I picked up a Beverly Cleary book about Ramona, Jason grabbed it out of my hand and said, "That goes right here!" He tucked it neatly back on his shelf. He did the same with Matt Christopher sports books, Donald Sobol's Encyclopedia Brown books, and his current fad — Mad Libs. He also grabbed the Shel Silverstein books *Where the Sidewalk Ends* and *The Light in the Attic*. In fact, he put Shel Silverstein's books on his bedside table because he reads himself to sleep with the giggle-producing verses. When we finished, Jason's bookshelves reflected his interests, his age, and his reading ability.

Jason's mom and dad both worked; it was hard to make ends meet with three kids. They didn't have money to waste, so when they bought a book they wanted to make sure it was one Jason would like for a long time and would read over and over. No family can own all the books a child should read, so the Carleys, like other families, turned to the library because it was free. Jason borrowed books from both the public library and his school library. When he bought a book, it was most often a paperback from a series he knew he liked.

Like most eight-year-olds, Jason had nonstop energy. He ran more often than he walked. He bounced on a bed instead of getting into it. He moved across a room like a streak of lightning and left a trail of pillows or papers in his tracks. He was interested in everything from guppies and snakes to outer space. He played softball, soccer, badminton, or anything you can throw, hit, kick, or catch — but he liked to be read to and to read alone. The only sure way I could get him to sit still was to read to him. When I read to him, he turned into an avid listener.

Jason was a reader for the simple reason that his parents had read to him. His mother read to him at night to quiet him down from high-speed activity to sleepy time. His dad read with him from nature magazines, fishing books, and hunting guides, because he was an outdoorsman. And I read to him as a special part of every visit. On Christmas Eve, I always read *The Polar Express* and *The Night Before Christmas* to keep him busy while Santa arranged gifts and surprises under the tree. Jason was also a reader because he read by himself and had discovered that reading was fun. When he read to his little sister, he would hold nine-month-old Trisha on his lap and read Mother Goose verses to her. Because his patience was as short as a firecracker fuse, he cut the session short if Trisha grabbed for the page or squirmed around too much. Jason was beginning to pass the torch, a love of reading, that had been handed down to him.

During the week of babysitting, I chose *My Brother Sam Is Dead* by James Lincoln Collier and Christopher Collier as the book to read aloud to Kali and Jason. It's a compelling story narrated by the younger brother of a Revolutionary

War soldier — a book that would keep eleven-year-old Kali interested and yet not be too complex for Jason to understand. We read every night at bedtime, but we still had about three chapters to finish when it was time for me to go to the airport. Along with my suitcase, Jason carried the book to the car. While their mother drove to the airport, I read aloud. While we waited at the terminal until it was time for me to board my plane, I read aloud. I felt frazzled as I ran down the ramp to the plane. I chuckled when their mother called to say she had to finish reading the few remaining pages to Kali and Jason at the airport before they started home. That convinced me that Janie is taking her place in handing down the magic. It also convinced me that my grandchildren are growing up as readers who are hooked by a good story. I am thankful that I'm the grandmother and don't need to cope with all that energy twenty-four hours a day, seven days a week, twelve months a year!

Making a Reader out of Your Seven- or Eight-year-old

My granddaughter Kali is now a teacher. She wrote to me about a student she helped tutor in summer school.

Dear Grandma,
Billy was in the second grade and did not like to read at all. His mom told me that he also was not "very good" at reading and she thought that's why he didn't read much. It was a vicious cycle — he didn't read much because he wasn't good at it, yet he couldn't practice to get good at it, because he didn't like to read.
Anyway, I began using "academic" incentives with him, to get him to at least try to read with me. We would play memory games with flash cards that had

both a picture and the word on them. After he began to master the words on the cards with the picture and the word, we moved to flash cards that just had the word on them. Although he was doing well at recognizing the words, he began to get bored with the same game. We then moved to sentences. He used the same flash cards as before, but instead of just matching them together, he began to put sentences together. At first, he made sentences with three words, then four, five and so on. It became a challenge for him to think of the longest sentence he could! After a week or two of sentence building, he came up with the idea of adding on to the flash cards sentences with his own imaginative thoughts. His thoughts then became more sentences, and longer sentences, until he was finally writing stories. He found a love for writing and then for reading because he wanted to share his stories with others by READING to them!

This is just a brief version of the progress he went through to achieve his success and love for reading. The entire process actually lasted only a few months, with tutoring only occurring two days a week. Overall, though, it really was an amazing success story and I can just imagine how much he is reading and writing today!
Love,
Kali

As they learn to read on their own, seven- and eight-year-olds begin the transition from picture books to chapter books without illustrations. This is an easy change for most, and some, pumped up by their own reading success, may even look at simple picture books as babyish. Other children may find the transition more difficult. Without the colorful illustrations, a page may seem stark and unwelcoming. We all enjoy pictures. Otherwise, art museums would close and *National Geographic* would be out of business. If your child is having trouble making the leap from an artist's illustrations to the purely imaginative pictures a reader creates in his head, you can help by asking what your child imagines when a passage is read. Encourage your child to draw illustrations to go along with a story or to describe scenes he sees in his mind's eye. Let him know that whatever he comes up with is just fine — perfect, in fact, since he's taken over as the illustrator now.

Here are suggestions for seven- and eight-year-olds:

1. *Follow your child's interests.* If your child likes to use the computer at school, get books and magazines on computers. If she is interested in bugs, get books on bugs. If she likes to jump rope, get books of jump-rope rhymes.

2. *Share books you enjoyed as a child.* If your parents read to you, find the same books to read to your child. There is a special magic in hearing books from the good old days that you read when you were a little girl or boy. Robert Louis Stevenson's poetry is a good place to start.

3. *Get a collection of fairy tales.* Look for illustrated versions of individual tales. Interest in fairy tales peaks around seven or eight; children of this age think it is poetic justice when the Big Billy Goat butts the Troll off the bridge and into the water. Their sense of fair play will change later, but this is the last time fairy tales speak so clearly to them.

4. *Find riddle and joke books.* Seven- and eight-year-olds have a weird or bizarre sense of humor. They like elephant jokes, gross punch lines, and jokes that make adults groan. Let them read their jokes aloud to you and try to catch you on the riddles while you're washing the dishes.

5. *Find books about sports stars and heroes.* Have the books

available when the hero appears on television so you can capitalize on the current interest by reading more about the person.

6. *Get a craft book.* Make a project together. We found a book on dinosaurs that had cutouts for us to make. Now we've found rocket ships and paper dolls.

7. *Use a cookbook together.* Make a recipe of a favorite food. After you read Laura Ingalls Wilder's *The Little House in the Big Woods*, get *The Little House Cookbook*, which has all the recipes for food mentioned in the series.

8. *Find an interactive book.* Some books allow the reader to make choices about the next section to read. Let your child read her chosen path to you, then you read your choice to her.

9. *Arrange for your seven- or eight-year-old to read to a younger child.* This additional practice improves his reading fluency and helps him see the joy in sharing books with others. It also raises self-esteem.

10. *Find books about things around you.* During the week I spent with three of my grandchildren, we took a walk every day because that was one way to keep them entertained. Because the family lives out in the country, we walked along a quiet country road taking turns pushing Trisha in her stroller. On the day their parents were coming home, we collected bouquets of weed flowers and wildflowers to fill vases for every room. We found Aliki's book *A Weed Is a Flower* to identify the goldenrod, Queen Anne's lace, touch-me-nots, and thistles we had collected.

11. *Prepare a time capsule for your family.* Use a small box to prepare a time capsule that reflects information about your family. Help your child put small objects into the box that, when put together, reveal important things about your family. You might include photographs, recipes of favorite foods, letters

from special people, an unmatched sock, a ribbon or hair clip, some jacks, a ball, an autograph book, a school report, or a drawing. Put the box away somewhere for an agreed-upon length of time, after which you'll open it together.

Making a Writer out of Your Seven- or Eight-year-old

Seven- and eight-year-old children do not distinguish totally between drawing and writing to tell a story. They draw pictures, label them, and regard the whole construction as a story. As they develop more control over the ability to express themselves in words, they rely less on illustration and more on words to tell their stories.

Good writers read a lot. They get ideas about how to shape their own writing from reading the work of other people. In one of Jason's own stories, you can see the influence of both books and firsthand experience. You will also notice some invented spelling — spelling words the way they sound to him, such as "caricders" for characters and "stachu of liperte" for Statue of Liberty. As much as we may be tempted to pressure young children to revise their work to get it "right," as adult writers do, beginning writers are generally impatient with revisions. They write it once and that's it! Telling the story is their priority and, at this stage, it's more important to keep the joy and creativity flowing than to turn writing into an unpleasant chore. This, then, is Jason's first (and only) draft.

Caricders by Jason Russell Ream
One day Cathy was reading a book and all of the sudden the caricders jumped out of the book. And the book was called A Kid's Guide to New York City. And the stachu of liperte was the tallist

thing that came out of the book. It walked down the street and some people freaked out because they didn't think the stachu of liperte could walk. All the kids liked the stachu of liperte and they played the hole day with him at the park. The stachu of liperte didn't have his candel lit so a boy went home to get some machts to lite it. And he came back with some machts and lit his candel. After he came down, the stachu of liperte was on fire. They all ran. The fire was so bad that the houses got on fire. And Cathy put the fire out. And everbody said she was a hero. The end.

Jason will eventually learn to spell words correctly as he continues to read, write, and study spelling in school. Just as a child learns to read by reading, so does he learn to write by writing. Here are some activities for your child to make writing real and to keep it fun.

Tips for Making Your Child a Writer

1. *Keep a journal as you read.* Encourage your child to write down thoughts at the end of a chapter. Try to predict what will happen next in the episode.

2. *Write a thank-you letter.* Whenever Grandma or Aunt Sara remembers a birthday or holiday, have your child write them a note to say thanks.

3. *Create your own cards.* Make your own valentines with your child. Write invitations to a birthday party or for any occasion.

4. *Keep score at sports events.* Teach your child to keep score at a Little League game or a basketball game. Use a list of

the players to keep track of the number of points each player scores.

5. *Write a letter to an author.* Write a letter to a favorite author. Mention good books and what your child thought about them. Your child can tell about himself and what he likes to read. Send the letter to the publisher.

6. *Write a letter from one character to another.* Have your child write a letter from one of her favorite characters to another. For example, have Ramona Quimby write to Encyclopedia Brown.

7. *Make up jokes and write them down.* Jokes can be fun as your child learns. Jokes clearly demonstrate that words need to appear in a certain order to achieve an effect. If the child gets the words mixed up in telling a joke, people just look confused. If he tells the joke correctly, people laugh. The reward is instant and gratifying.

It may require supreme patience on your part to play along when your child tells you a thousand corny jokes, but find some consolation in the thought that these deceptively silly jokes can offer valuable language instruction.

8. *Create a newspaper.* Create a family newspaper about your own family. Write feature articles about big family events. Write headlines about family news and special events: "Welcome Home!" or "Happy Birthday!"

9. *Do crossword puzzles.* People who work crossword puzzles become wordsmiths — they pay attention to words. Do crossword puzzles with your child, asking, for example, "What is a three-letter word for feline?" Children learn that words have more than one meaning; they learn definitions and they pay attention to the lengths and the sounds of words. All these skills learned in fun serve them well as readers and writers.

10. *Create a family book.* Help your child make a book about

your family's history or cultural heritage. Draw a picture of your family tree with spaces for parents, brothers, sisters, grandparents, great-grandparents, aunts, uncles, and cousins. List the dates that members of the family came to America from another country. Make a separate page for each holiday you celebrate and write the things that your family does to make that day special. List the foods you prepare, the decorations you put up, and the gifts you give. Be sure to include everyone's birthday, Christmas, Kwanzaa, or Hanukkah, Thanksgiving, Halloween, and Valentine's Day. Patricia Reilly Giff has written *All About Stacy* in which Stacy constructs an "About Me" box. Get ideas about making your own.

11. *Communicate with notes.* For fun, the whole family can observe a period of silence when all communication is accomplished by passing notes.

Tips for Busy Parents

1. *Get informational books and series books.* Children like both informational and fantasy books in a series. Seven- and eight-year-old children are curious about everything in their world. They want to know how the world works, how things grow, and how their bodies function. You can build on this curiosity by giving them informational books that appeal to them. Joanna Cole and Bruce Degen provide some wonderful experiences with science in The Magic School Bus series. *The Magic School Bus in the Time of the Dinosaurs, The Magic School Bus Inside a Beehive, The Magic School Bus Inside a Hurricane,* and others, provide accurate scientific information in a humorous and engaging way. Mary Pope Osborne creates an appealing collection of fact, farce, and fantasy stories called The Magic Tree House series. Readers respond to clever titles, such as *Dinosaurs Before Dark, Mummies in the Morning,* and *Night of*

the Ninjas. Her mysterious tone and fast-paced stories have plenty of suspense, magic, and information to please science lovers.

2. *Prepare book-related snacks.* When children arrive home from school, they walk in the door, they throw down their backpacks and their coats, and then they want a snack. Involve them in preparing healthy snacks and put a poem or book beside the snacks; they will read as they nibble. Roald Dahl's *Revolting Recipes* includes recipes for Snozzcumbers and Fresh Mudburgers. They all sound disgusting but taste surprisingly good. *Brown Bear* cookies and *Where the Wild Things Are* wild rice cakes are just the beginning of snack recipes you and your child can create.

3. *Start a memory book.* Kids are collectors. They'll collect anything: tiny cars, Pokémon cards, Disney World pins, key chains, Beanie Babies, Arthur characters, stamps, or newspaper clippings. Let your child choose a subject of interest, get a composition book and a glue stick, and start clipping related items. Autumn leaves, bird feathers, newspaper articles, and photographs of their favorite sports star all make good memory book material. They will read to select items, they will write labels, and they will reread many times as they treasure their collection. My grandson Jason now keeps a scrapbook of newspaper clippings about his cross-country team events.

4. *Make holiday greeting cards.* Many holidays and birthdays call for greeting cards. Children can write the invitations to their birthday party, send relatives holiday greetings, send cards to children in an orphanage and to elderly people in nursing homes. The people who receive them appreciate a child's efforts more than a commercial card.

5. *Write to family members.* Not all letters and thank-you cards need to be mailed to people far away. If two children have a disagreement, after the dust settles suggest that they

write apologies to each other. Remind them that writing allows the time and opportunity to choose just the right words they want to say. A thank-you card to Dad for cooking a special dinner, to Mom for a trip to the museum, or to both parents for hosting the birthday party are all real opportunities for writing.

6. *Interview parents or grandparents.* Help your child make up a list of questions to ask of parents or grandparents. Tape-record the interviews so your child can listen again to their comments and stories about what happened when they were her age. She can write stories about their experiences.

7. *Explore family letters, albums.* Most people have old packs of letters held together with rubber bands or tied with ribbons. Allow your child to go through the letters to see what your family was doing at those dates. Encourage her to write a story about what was happening in your family based on the old letters. Look through a family album. Describe family events pictured in the photograph albums. Find poems that go with the photographs and arrange poems and pictures together.

8. *Write it down.* If you're on the telephone or busy concentrating on something else and your child can't wait to tell you what happened, suggest that he write it down and read it to you later.

Did You Know . . .

- Children follow their parents' examples. If they see you relax in front of television, they will, too. If they see you read, they will, too.
- Praise works better than punishment; accentuate the positive things your child does. It helps build self-confidence, which leads to more success.
- Problem-solving is the brain's favorite exercise.

- Children need to know that you are interested in their school. Attend parent meetings, visit their classrooms.
- Keep in touch with school.
- Children spend an average of 500 hours a year in a car; a few years ago, it was 200 hours. Keep books in the car.
- Most poets had an adult who fed them beautiful language as a child; often it was a parent.
- A child will take the same book that was read to him and begin reading it himself.
- Ten minutes of freely chosen reading at home makes a big improvement in a child's performance on reading tests at school.
- Children learn to become better readers by writing.
- Writing leads to reading.
- Thirty percent of the nation's largest companies (and many of its smaller ones) are collectively paying $25 billion a year to teach remedial math and reading to entry-level employees.
- No new inventions would ever be created without imagination. Reading helps to develop children's imagination.
- Voracious readers are made, not born. Children who read most, read best.
- Children still need to be read to after they learn to read on their own. They need to hear what good reading sounds like.

Chapter 8: Nine- and Ten-year-olds

Life with Nine- and Ten-Year-Olds

Nine-year-olds:
- Develop best friends
- Play sports
- Enjoy series books
- Choose informational books
- Are fascinated with strange but true facts (such as in *The Guinness Book of World Records*)
- Like mysteries
- Prefer realistic stories over fairy tales
- Like happy endings
- Want sophisticated chapter books and real novels
- Have a weird sense of humor
- Like gross, corny jokes

Eva is nine years old, in the third grade, and has a brother, Philip, who is two years older. Eva is a cat lover. Tigger, her cat, meets her at the door when she comes home from school. Eva says, "Tigger really counts as a kid. She's the cutest kitten in the whole world." Therefore, Tigger gets the first hug, Mom gets the second. Then it's snack time, talk time to tell Mother the exciting things that happened at school, and hurry-up time to get ready for the next event.

Eva's life outside school is heavily scheduled five days a week. Monday it's dancing class, Tuesday and Thursday are religious school lessons, Wednesday it's piano lessons, and Friday it's Brownies. Mom is chauffeur for all events. When they return, Eva goes to her room to do her homework. She makes short work of her assignments so she has time to watch TV before supper.

Eva has lots of friends. She says, "My best friends are Melissa, Lauren, Jamie, Iya, Kyoko, Nachi, and Yuko," naming every girl in her class at school. "I call them up on the telephone all the time."

Eva keeps a reading journal for books she reads; she records the title, the author, the date she starts and the date she finishes, the number of pages she reads each day, and what the book is about. Eva says, "I love Roald Dahl books, series books like the Boxcar Children, Dear America, American Girl, and Sweet Valley Twins and Sweet Valley Kids. Oh, and Laura Ingalls Wilder, she's my favorite. I like really long books."

Eva wrote in her autobiography at school:

> *"Someone special in my life is Omy and Opa. Omy and Opa are very close to me. They are like a third pair of grandparents. Omy makes the best milk shakes in the world. Every time we went to their house, she would ask me what kind of ice cream I wanted and she always had it. Vanilla ice cream. They even had straws called spoon straws; they're little spoons with straws attached to them. Now we don't see Omy and Opa anymore because they moved to Louisiana. I shure do miss them."*

Roberto organizes everything, especially his baseball cards and his lunch. Every night, he packs his granola bar and makes sure that his fruit drink is strawberry and that the bread for his sandwich is "super fresh." At school, he likes the way his teacher talks to him and listens to him. "It's like home," he says, giving his mom a smile. When he comes home, he checks in, then darts out to see Cody Garcia, one of his *amigos*. "Cody eats onions," Roberto tells his father, who always reminds him about the importance of having a balanced meal. On Thursdays after school, Roberto has his cello lessons. He takes his music seriously. "Practice, practice," he sings out while his fingers go through the scales. Roberto also loves to in-line skate, swim, and play pool.

In the evening after homework, Roberto likes to play with his action figures while he watches TV. Or he lies down on the sofa and reads *Calvin and Hobbes* and laughs out loud. *Hobbes is smart*, he mumbles to himself. Roberto's eyes open wide when he talks about his favorite comic book characters. As bedtime approaches, he asks his mother, "Can I camp out tonight?" This means he wants to sleep in his sleeping bag in his room. There he will double-check all his recent baseball card purchases and trades, tally his cards, and carefully add them to his shoe-box files in alphabetical order. After his mother finishes reading him his bedtime stories, she makes sure she closes his door gently and hangs Roberto's crayon sign for all to read — PRIVATE: KEEP OUT.

Ten-year-olds:
- Take pride in their developing talents
- Read biographies about real people
- Like adventures with real heroes
- Like funny books such as *How to Eat Fried Worms* by Thomas Rockwell
- Develop lasting friendships
- Are fascinated by video games
- Begin to e-mail and instant message with friends.
- Enjoy active sports and bike riding

David is a pet lover; he has nineteen pets including hermit crabs, crayfish, newts, and turtles. When he goes to the library, he gets reptile books only. He has read a magazine called *Nintendo Power*, and Roald Dahl's books *The Twits* and *James and the Giant Peach*. But he specializes in books about his pets. The big fish tank is in the living room; terrariums are in the dining room and in his bedroom. He feeds his pets before school and helps clean the tanks when they need it.

David's family is Chinese American and runs the local cleaners. Every day after school, David and his brother, Sam, help at the store. Every Friday, David and Sam go to their grandmother's house in the city; they return on Sunday afternoon. David says, "My grandmother fixes me special food like rice, noodles, dumplings, and soup. She tells me stories like 'The Boy Who Cried Wolf,' 'Peter and the Wolf,' and stories about Jesus. I don't know how she remembers everything, but she knows 'em all. Nobody reads to me, I can do it myself."

On Wednesday, David has a math tutor and on Saturday, he goes to math school near his grandmother's house. David is outstanding in math and says he goes to math school "just because my dad wants me to." One time David found that he had left his homework at his home instead of taking it with him to his grandmother's. His older cousin drove thirty miles in the middle of the night to retrieve the forgotten homework; there's a great deal of family support to see that David does well, especially in math. When David and Sam are at their grandmother's, they do not go outside to play with neighborhood children. They play indoors with their cousins, watch TV, listen to Grandma's stories, and do homework. Like all children, David is learning his family's values and cultural heritage.

Making a Reader out of Your Nine- or Ten-Year-Old

Nine- and ten-year-olds are active and curious, and are full of-life energy machines. They do not sit around waiting for something to happen, they make things happen. They become excited about projects if you are excited about them.

Male influences are especially important during these years. On average, 88 percent of elementary school teachers are female, so boys depend heavily on their fathers as role models; girls simply idolize them. If children think Dad is only interested in sports, that's what they will work on hardest. If they think Dad values reading and computer skills, they will try to excel in those areas.

Charley's dad is an outdoorsman, and the two of them track animals, spot wild geese, hunt, and camp out. With his dad's encouragement, Charley reads outdoor adventure and survival stories like *Hatchet* and *Tracker*, both by Gary Paulsen. To encourage your nine- and ten-year-olds to read:

1. *Take your child to the library.* Help your child feel comfortable at the library. Help him locate the kind of books he likes and show him how to search for informational books on topics of interest. Show your child that you are interested in books, too. When a child sees a parent or older brother or sister checking out books, he will follow their lead. A library is an impressive place, a dynamic monument to the importance of books. It's hard not to get caught up in the excitement of reading when you're surrounded by so many books and so many enthusiastic readers. Libraries supplement their book collections with computers, story readings, colorful posters, and exhibits to make a visit even more appealing.

2. *Get how-to books.* Nine- and ten-year-olds like to be involved in building projects. Get books on how to build a birdhouse, a tree house, swings, model airplanes, or boats.

3. *Work together on building projects.* Nothing is as rewarding for a child as working on a project with dad or mom. Building anything is more fun when you work together. Children can

read the instructions but may need you to look over their shoulders. The results — totally successful or not — show them that it is important to read carefully.

4. *Start a collection.* Nine- and ten-year-olds are also collectors. They collect baseball cards, football cards, soccer cards, and cards of comic-book superheroes. Get books on collecting cards. Bruce Brooks, a noted author of books for adolescents, is certain that his son, Alexander, learned to read by collecting soccer cards. Alexander memorized players' averages and records. He studied the cards, kept them in his room, and carried some of them with him at all times. He liked to surprise his dad with amazing facts and figures he learned from his soccer cards.

5. *Enjoy comic strips and comic books.* Comic books may not be classic literature, but most adults don't spend all their time reading Shakespeare, either. Dilbert is a current hit of many grown-ups; and Gary Larsen's offbeat cartoon books and calendars have long been popular with adults. Reading should be fun. Read the Sunday comics together. Archie comic books have been rated as first-grade reading-level material, but Batman comics average about a sixth-grade reading level. For a child still learning to read, the illustrations provide a direct visual link to the words.

6. *Decorate a T-shirt.* Many people become walking billboards when they put on T-shirts. Let your child make a statement about herself — instead of wearing a commercial statement — by making her own T-shirt, using waterproof felt-tipped markers. Create a slogan, a scene, or a caricature of a favorite character. Creativity counts.

7. *Read part of a book aloud.* Get your child started on a book by reading enough of it aloud to get him hooked on the story. Chances are, he'll finish it by himself. I am purposefully

using the male pronoun here; it is more often boys than girls at this age who prefer active sports over reading to fill up their time.

My son, Webb, was not much of a voluntary reader at age ten. He was required to do a book report for school once a month and so he read one book each month — usually the night before the report was due. He always looked for skinny books with lots of pictures. He gave reports on every sports star imaginable because he could use information he gained from the sports pages and TV and wouldn't need to read the book at all. He finally did read a book, however. It was *Toward Morning* by Maia Wojciechowska, about the uprising in Poland during World War II. I got him started on the book by reading the first part of it aloud to him. He was fascinated by the secret missions young people worked in to undercut the political forces taking over Poland. I read several chapters aloud before he finally was hooked and said, "Give it to me." He read the rest alone. He used that same book for book reports during the fourth grade, fifth grade, sixth grade, and seventh grade. Today he reads computer magazines, business analyses, and, once in a while, a book of political intrigue — a lingering effect, perhaps, of his rare connection with *Toward Morning* so many years ago. I wish that as a young mother, I had known then what I know now. There were plenty of books he would have liked if I had gotten him hooked as a reader.

Making a Writer out of Your Nine- or Ten-year-old

Nines and tens have gained reasonable control over the mechanics of writing. They have moved beyond manuscript printing to cursive writing. They are able to write for half an hour or more without getting writers' cramps or tired fingers. Many of them write on computers. They see the practical value of writing and will write on their own if it is valued by others around them.

1. *Make lists.* Ask your child to write down the items you need from the grocery store by calling them out as you check the cupboards and refrigerator. Make a list of the relatives who are coming for a holiday so you know how many places to set. Make place cards for a family dinner. Make a list of the friends to be invited to a birthday party. Make a list of the books you have read together. Make a list about anything; your child enjoys it and gets writing practice.

2. *Make a book.* Some nine- and ten-year-olds help with babysitting, especially for younger siblings. Help your son make an alphabet or counting book to use with the younger child. Make a secret wish book, a grandma book, a grandpa book. Make a shape book — in the shape of a train or a dog. Make a pop-up book with flaps to lift and figures that rise up. They can use these to entertain younger charges.

3. *Write a letter to an author.* Have your child tell the author what he likes or wants to know about that author's books. Here is a letter from a fan of J. K. Rowling's Harry Potter books:

> *Dear J. K. Rowling,*
> *I must say, the book Harry Potter was unlike any book I have read before. In every other book I have read, the witches and wizards are the villains and the people more like you and me are the people who are right. In your book, the witches and wizards are the good people and the people more like you and me are the bad people. That is one detail that makes this story so unique. The way you describe the setting*

and what is going on made it easy for me to create
pictures in my mind.
Thank you for writing Harry Potter.
Sincerely,
Katie Wooten
North Shore Schools
Glen Head, New York

4. *Write new verses.* Have your child use a familiar song or tune to write new verses about his family. Use a limerick form of verse and write new words, such as "There once was a girl who was nine . . ."

5. *Rewrite a story or tale.* Suggest that your child read a story, close the book, and rewrite it in her own words. There are many ways to tell a story and the art of writing is in choosing your own words.

6. *Keep a journal.* Children need to learn that their lives are worth writing about. Keeping a journal about what they do, what they think, how they feel, or what they read is a good way to help them value their own experiences and feel good about themselves. Have them read some autobiographies written by their favorite sports star or author. They find that the simple details about people are very interesting.

7. *Play word games.* Boggle and Scrabble are games that require players to combine letters to create words. These games are fun and develop spelling skills and increase vocabulary. The game Royalty is a card game about making words. Balderdash, a commercial version of an old parlor game we always called the Dictionary Game, asks players to try to fool one another by making up convincing definitions for obscure words. One learns new words and gets practice in creative writing. These games are good for developing

language skills and for engaging the whole family in an entertaining activity.

8. *Prepare a poetry palette.* Just as a painter collects and arranges colors and textures for his art, a poet collects and arranges words for his poems. Have your child list words about his favorite foods, smells, clothes, places. Make a list of "I wish," "I remember," "I wonder" statements. Collect comparisons —"The crescents of my toenails are like tiny moons," or "Father wakes up from his nap like a hibernating bear in springtime." Have him choose words from his palette to write a poem.

Tips for Busy Parents

One summer, my niece Jessica and my granddaughter Kali came for a visit. I was surprised to discover that nine-year-old Jessica was a much better reader than ten-year-old Kali. When we read before bedtime, Jessica zoomed through a book while Kali labored over a few pages. One day, I tried a technique that really helped. We were reading Lois Lowry's *Anastasia at Your Service*, and I had Jessica read the words that Anastasia said and Kali read the words that another character, Anastasia's friend, said. I read the parts in between. The context, or the meaning of the story, seemed to carry Kali along. She read the dialogue smoothly and with expression because she understood what was happening in the story.

1. *Read one character's dialogue, have your child read another's.* Children read more easily when what they are reading makes sense to them. Dialogue is easier to read than descriptive paragraphs. Assign or choose parts, let your child become one of the characters and read the words that character says. Some people call this readers' theater. Just

have fun and read the parts; it helps bring books and characters to life.

2. *Read riddles or make them up.* Nine- and ten-year-olds love to be in the know. Have them read riddles and try to stump you. What has four wheels and flies? (A garbage truck.) Feed me and I live; give me water and I die. What am I? (Fire.) Write riddles or make them up for a talking game when you are driving along or preparing a meal. Read J. Patrick Lewis's *Riddle-Lightful*.

3. *Play thinking games.* Twenty questions of animal, vegetable, or mineral works for more mature youngsters. Jeopardy, in which you give the answer first and they respond with the appropriate question (You: "I am called the "father of our country." Child: "Who is George Washington?"), works for even more mature children. Once you start a game, your child will think up variations to make it unique.

4. *Work on projects.* Kids are continually bringing home projects they need to do. Whether it is for the school science fair, the scouts, or the religion teacher, pitch in and help. This doesn't mean that you do the project for your children, but it is more fun for everybody when you get involved. I helped build volcanoes, carve wooden cars, build model airplanes, create a model of the solar system, and dress a Pilgrim doll, among other things, to get our kids through school.

5. *Support scout activities.* If your child is a scout, participate in special events and help at home with scout projects. The Boy Scouts of America and the Girl Scouts of America created a "Reading Badge." The badge can be earned by reading to people who cannot read, collecting books for people who do not have them, and supporting reading activities in the community.

6. *Write fractured fairy tales.* Nines and tens are a little beyond the traditional fairy-tale story. Use the stories to

write a parody, a new version, a modern news story about the characters, or headlines about the events. Write a lost-and-found column for items depicted in the fairy tales, such as a spinning wheel, a glass slipper, or a pocketful of crumbs. Jon Scieszka's *The True Story of the Three Little Pigs* is a good example of having fun with a familiar story.

7. *Create a camera story.* Photo essays are popular reading material. Help children create their own. Decide on a topic and tell the story in photographs. Digital cameras shorten the waiting time between the idea and the finished product. Photographs of your child as a baby are immensely satisfying. Use duplicates to create an autobiography in pictures and words.

8. *Write the text for wordless books.* Your child is old enough to create dialogue for characters in wordless books. Write on little balloon-shaped pieces of paper (Post-its work fine) and stick them above the characters. Write on strips of paper and attach them to each page to tell what is happening in the pictures. You can make a game by keeping the strips loose and having your child match them to the right picture. Tana Hoban, Denise Fleming, David McPhail, and Chris Raschka create fascinating wordless books. If you buy wordless books in paperback, cut up a copy and see if your child can put it back in the proper sequence. Or you and your child can experiment by rearranging the pages to see how the same story can be told in different ways or how a completely different story can emerge from a new arrangement of pages.

Did You Know . . .

- Children like to read what *they* choose to read — not what others choose for them.
- Students who read a lot have more background knowledge and are more curious about the world.

- Problem-solving is to the brain what aerobic exercise is to the body.
- Children will read magazine articles on topics that interest them. Those interested in animals read nature magazines; those interested in computers read *Nintendo Power*.
- A number of studies show that more top students (nearly 100 percent) in all grades read comic strips or comic books than did lower-ranking students.
- Students in grades three through twelve learn about 3,000 new words a year. They learn the majority of new words incidentally while reading.
- Voracious readers are made, not born. No child is born loving baseball or pizza; they learn to like what they see their parents liking.
- Children who read most also read best, according to national tests of reading ability.
- Most avid readers go through a stage of reading "series" books. Although the series may not qualify as high-quality literature, all that reading practice helps develop speed and fluency.
- Research shows that if time is allotted for reading in school, kids will also read at home. See if your school allows time for independent reading.

Chapter 9: Eleven- and Twelve-Year-Olds

Life with Eleven- and Twelve-year-olds

Eleven-year-olds:
- Like boys (girls), and like girls (boys)
- Listen to popular music
- Like to dance to popular music
- Enjoy horror movies and stories
- Like mysteries, such as Nancy Drew
- Read series books, The Sisterhood of the Traveling Pants, Harry Potter, Dear America, American Girl
- Attach more importance to friendship
- Like babies and little kids
- Talk on the telephone and instant message as much as allowed
- Write notes to friends
- Memorize poetry and song lyrics
- Like to ice-skate, in-line skate
- Like basketball, football, baseball, all sports
- Read about people just a little older than they are
- Read teenage magazines (*Teen People*, J-14), and fashion magazines
- Like animals and animal stories, especially horse stories
- Like survival and adventure stories
- Like happy endings to stories
- Imitate their friends in dress and behavior
- Begin to develop an interest in science fiction

Ten-year-old Trisha Becomes a Fifteen-year-old Reader

My daughter, Janie, recently wrote to me about her daughter Trisha:

> Dear Mom,
>
> This letter is just to update you on how your reading to me as a child has been passed on and touched your granddaughter's life. My fifteen-year-old daughter, Trisha, is still reading daily, even though her tastes have changed over the years.
>
> When she was ten, Trisha's favorite book was Sky Rider *by Nancy Springer. She also loved* My Side of the Mountain, Julie's Wolf Pack, *and* Julie of the Wolves *by Jean Craighead George. Trisha would read these books over and over, actually memorizing most of them. Jason liked the same books so we had to get two copies from the library or buy two copies.*
>
> Among her other favorite books was Upchuck and the Rotten Willy *and any books about dogs. One of her passions is animals, especially dogs and horses. I always buy her an animal book for each holiday so we have a whole series now. She has reread several of them, because she loves them. She also got interested in Madeleine L'Engle's* Wrinkle in Time. *Virginia Hamilton's* Sweet Whisper, Brother Rush, *Katherine Paterson's* Bridge to Terabithia, *and Elizabeth Baity's* Ginger Pye, *which she wanted me to read. Then she wanted her sister, Kali, to read it, because she just loved it.*
>
> Now that she's in the middle of the teenage years, fifteen thinking about twenty-one, she is more selective in her reading choices. Her favorite books now are

The Life of Pi *by Yann Martel, the Harry Potter series by J. K. Rowling,* Lord of the Rings *by Tolkien,* Life Is Funny *by E. R. Frank and* The Secret Life of Bees *by Sue Monk Kidd.*

Anyways, thanks for teaching me to love reading; it has been handed down to your granddaughter. It takes us to another place and you are able to forget any problems or stress that you had to deal with in the day, it helps you relax.
Love,
Janie

"I cleaned my son's room the other night and noticed a little spiral notebook I had gotten for him to keep his assignments in," says Linda, a mother of an eleven-year-old boy. "The notebook was filled so I asked him if he needed a new one and he said, 'I didn't really use it for assignments. Go ahead and look at it if you want.' He had copied down lines of poetry by William Butler Yeats, lyrics from Elvis Costello, Paul Simon, and Randy Newman songs, and a few poems from a book by Mel Glenn. I was fascinated so I kept reading. I found some poems that were not credited to any poet so I asked him, 'Who wrote these?' His answer, 'I did,' astounded me. I had no idea that he was interested in reading poetry, let alone that he was trying to write poetry."

Twelve-year-olds:
- Like pop, country, rap, rock and roll, and heavy metal music
- Participate in all kinds of sports
- Begin to specialize in some sport
- Like physical activity
- Eat like horses and are bottomless pits

- Begin informal dating, mostly in groups
- Read fashion and teenage magazines
- Like American history in fact and fiction
- Like horror stories and movies
- Like comedy, fantasy, and science fiction
- Watch TV sitcoms or reality shows from thirty minutes to six hours a day
- Are very interested in their social lives
- Are interested in clothes and hairstyles
- Are interested in makeup (girls)
- Spend endless hours on the telephone and computer with friends
- Have mood swings; seem grown-up one minute, a child the next
- Like to do things for themselves

Jared, in the sixth grade, is a black belt in karate. On Monday, he teaches karate to younger children. On Tuesday and Thursday, he goes to karate lessons. On Wednesday, he goes to Hebrew School. On Friday, he teaches another class in karate. Jared reads nonfiction karate books. Needless to say, karate is important to Jared.

The girls in Jared's classroom consider him attractive. The boys turn to him as a leader in sports, dress, hairstyles, and behavior. His teacher, Ed Conti, says, "Fortunately, Jared is a good kid." Jared comes to the school yard to play sports before or after his karate sessions. He tells disapprovingly about some kids who blew up their family mailbox with firecrackers last Fourth of July. Jared's big brother is his model; he has inherited lots of his big brother's clothes and his values. Jared chooses to read karate books primarily, but when Mr. Conti read aloud from Gary Paulsen's *Hatchet*, Jared got the book and read ahead on his own. Like many other twelve-year-old boys, Jared is interested in many things; he follows up on books that strike his interests.

Kaelan writes free-verse poetry and has been keeping a journal for the past three years. Her favorite poets are Emily Dickinson, Langston Hughes, and Maya Angelou. In terms of novels, she loves to read everything from Stephen King to historical fiction.

Reading was not always such a pleasure for Kaelan; she had problems in the beginning. Unlike many children, she was not able to make a smooth transition from listening to books to reading them herself. Not everybody learns the same way. Her concerned parents tried to help her. Although she struggled to read simple books, they continued to read challenging books aloud to her. The more she struggled, the more they read. In second grade, as Kaelan continued to fall behind most of her classmates in reading skills, an assessment revealed that the cause of her reading problems was dyslexia. Kaelan's reading skills were at a kindergarten level, but the people administering the test were astounded to find that her vocabulary skills were at a twelfth-grade level. She couldn't read many words, but because her parents had read so many books to her, she understood thousands of words and could use them in conversation. Kaelan took special classes to help her make better connections between the written letters and the sounds of written language and her reading ability steadily improved. Now, as a twelve-year-old, Kaelan still reads more slowly than she'd like, but she reads with exceptional comprehension. Among her heroes, Kaelan lists the Dalai Lama, Julie Taymor (the director of the staged version of *The Lion King*), and her parents who, by reading aloud to her, provided her with a storehouse of words and an appreciation of literature that she still draws upon.

Making a Reader out of Your Eleven- or Twelve-year-Old

Eleven- and twelve-year-olds have minds of their own; they think they are much more independent than they really are. It is frightening to realize that as parents we will soon have even less influence over their decisions than we have at this age. It is also frightening to know that outside demands on their time will increase as they move into the teenage years. Find the right book and you can turn a reluctant reader into an avid one. The Harry Potter series proved this statement to be true.

Some say that if children are not readers by the time they leave elementary school, they probably will never become avid readers. I don't exactly agree with this dire prediction, but I will say that if children never read or hear a really *good* book by the time they are teenagers, they're not likely to become readers.

Elevens and twelves listen to their friends and their teachers more readily than they listen to their parents. If a friend says a book is good, then it must be good. If a teacher reads aloud from a book at school, they want to get the book to read ahead, to follow along, or to reread the same book.

Preteens are social animals. They run in packs. They imitate their friends. They want to look like everybody else and do not want to stand out in a crowd in any way. Their clothes, their hairstyles, and the books they read must assure them they are part of the group.

Listening to music becomes an increasingly important part of many preteenagers' lives. We can all remember songs from our youth and the impact they had on us then — and even now when we hear those songs again. Popular songs are often written about young people, by young people, for young people. It's not surprising that these songs can strike a chord with your preteen; they speak his language and address feelings and issues your child might well be facing. Show interest in the music your child enjoys. Keep in mind that listening to songs is not so different from listening to poetry — the rhythms, the rhymes, the compact telling of a story. Remind your child that songs are written by somebody. Does the performer write her own songs, or is she singing someone else's words? Discuss the lyrics as you would any other piece of writing.

With the turbulent teenage years fast approaching, this can be a challenging time in a child's life, when he is facing difficult new issues and struggling with his independence. It's easy for kids to forget that their parents were ever young, and your preteen may start to question the authority (and intelligence) of his parents. Keep up with his interests and fads. Be aware of the peer pressures he is facing and let him know that he can talk with you about any problems. If he is too uncomfortable to discuss certain sensitive issues with you, offer him an appropriate book to bridge the gap and to serve as a starting point for conversation.

Here are some ways to continue to support the reading habits of your eleven- and twelve-year-old:

1. *Give a friend a book.* Give your child's friend a book you want your child to read. This may not be a very subtle move, but it works.

2. *Send a book to the teacher.* If you know a book that children of this age will enjoy, send it to the teacher with a request that it be read aloud to the group. Chances are that your child will want a copy, too.

3. *Subscribe to a teenage magazine.* Children want to read about people a couple of years older than they are. Teen magazines are just right. Children read them to practice what their lives will be like in a few years.

4. *Get books about their heroes.* Sports figures, dancers,

musicians, rock stars, TV stars, movie stars, authors, poets, scientists, and other modern-day heroes appear in books. Find the books at the library and sprinkle them in your preteenager's path.

5. *Start your child on series books.* When children read the first book in a series, they are anxious to find the second one. Harry Potter, *The Chronicles of Prydain*, *The Sisterhood of the Traveling Pants*, *The Lord of the Rings*, Nancy Drew, and *A Series of Unfortunate Events* are all fair game. Reading books in a series increases the amount a child reads, which increases fluency, comprehension, and vocabulary.

6. *Read a book to your child.* Elevens and twelves still enjoy listening to a good story. Choose a book you have heard about and say, "I've been wanting to read this book. How about if we read it together? I'll start."

7. *Find movies based on books.* As they become more social and independent, modern preteens like going to the movies. Find movies based on books. *Charlie and the Chocolate Factory*, *Chitty Chitty Bang Bang*, *Because of Winn-Dixie*, *Stuart Little*, *A Little Princess*, *The Lion, the Witch and the Wardrobe*, and many other books have been made into films. Once children have seen the movie, they'll want to read the book. After they've read the book, talk about the differences between the book and the movie. Discuss how movies and books are very different art forms, how they are similar, and how the child participates in very different ways in experiencing them.

8. *Suggest that your child read a book before seeing the movie version.* Talk with your child about the characters, how she pictures the scenes, and then go to a theater or rent the DVD or videotape. Have her compare her imaginative impressions with the movie version. Many people are disappointed in a movie version of a book they've read and liked. Your child will realize that a movie is just someone's interpretation of a piece

of writing, that it's no better or worse than hers, and that her own imaginative collaboration with an author can be more satisfying.

9. *Find music to accompany reading.* Ask your child to select music to play as background for reading a story or verses.

10. *Create a literary jackdaw.* A jackdaw is named for a bird that collects all sorts of objects in its nest. Help your child make a literary jackdaw by collecting objects related to a book. The items serve as an excellent way to give a report on a book.

Making a Writer out of Your Eleven- or Twelve-Year-Old

Young people of eleven and twelve can easily see through attempts to get them to write for the sake of writing. Make writing projects practical and meaningful. Adults write for real reasons, and preteens will write for reasons meaningful to them. Try to adapt writing needs to their interests and activities. Here are some suggestions you can make to your child.

1. *Be aware of how writing surrounds us.* Writing isn't just something your child does as a classroom assignment. Writing is everywhere: advertising, packaging, instructions for new appliances, phone bills, parking signs, TV shows, songs, movie dialogue, politicians' speeches, favorite comedians' routines. Look with your child at all the uses of writing.

2. *Keep a journal.* At this age, keeping a journal can be more than just telling what happened today. Putting thoughts and feelings into words can be a reflective, clarifying process; writing can help make sense of complex emotions. Several famous authors kept journals as teenagers; they draw from them for their current writing.

3. *Prepare a babysitter's kit.* Many elevens and twelves baby-

sit for young children. Help them prepare a kit they can take with them on babysitting jobs. Make a list of basic safety rules, steps to take in an emergency, and ways to entertain their charges.

4. *Write lyrics for a popular melody.* Encourage your child to use the characters and plot of a book as the basis for the lyrics to a favorite tune.

5. *Write rap lyrics.* Rap music is a popular form of rhyming verse. Write some rap verses with your child; be sure to observe rhythm and rhyme patterns.

6. *Make a literary map.* Use one story, such as Tolkien's *Lord of the Rings*, as the basis for the map. Ask your preteens to draw a map of the territory the characters travel. Have them use a map of the world to locate the setting of books they have read.

7. *Write a review.* Preteens like to know that their opinions are valued. Ask them to review books for their friends or for a review journal that publishes adolescents' reviews. Read young adult choices in the *Journal of Adolescent & Adult Literacy*, published by the International Reading Association, 800 Barksdale Road, Newark, DE 19714-8139.

8. *Make a crossword puzzle.* Suggest that your child use the characters, objects, and events from a book as the basis for a crossword puzzle. Make a standard crossbreak diagram to begin. Start filling in words from the book. Make up clues for the words.

9. *Create a time line.* Time lines help young people put events into chronological sequence. Show your child how to use the time line for his life, the works of one author, or historical events and related books. A time line of the books a child reads at various ages would be very interesting and would show how much reading tastes change over the years.

10. *Make an acrostic.* Show your child how to write the title

of a book down the side of a page along the margin. For each letter in the title, give a word that describes your feelings about the book, or give the name of a character, place, or event that figures in the book. Another possibility is to write a sentence that begins with each letter of the title.

11. *Write a picture book for younger children.* The story in a picture book is told through a combination of words and illustrations. Help your child to create a picture book to put into the babysitter's kit. Decide which words go on each page and illustrate the story. He can expand the story told in words by weaving a subplot into the illustrations. Hide objects in the illustrations for younger children to find.

12. *Write a sequel.* Follow a favorite character from a story by writing additional episodes with your child. Tell a story from a different character's point of view. Move backward or forward in time to tell what is happening to the characters. Set the story in a new setting, for example, your neighborhood. Add a new character to a story. For example, the fourth little pig is a girl who huffs and puffs and blows the brick house down. She asks why the three little pigs want to sit at home and miss all the fun and excitement going on outside in the world.

13. *Write a parody.* Show your child how to use a familiar folktale as the basis for a parody, a comic imitation of a well-known piece of literature. Author Jon Scieszka and illustrator Lane Smith have played with humorous variations of traditional stories. Look at *The True Story of the Three Little Pigs* and *The Stinky Cheese Man.*

14. *Read a book, then write a screenplay or a play.* Your child can cast it with favorite actors or friends. Discuss TV shows and movies in terms of writing. Remind your child that someone had to write all the clever lines those movie stars are saying.

15. *Write a poem from a name.* Write your child's or another person's name down the side of a page. Together think of

words to describe the person. Here's what one of my students at New York University wrote:

B is for Brenda, black, beautiful, bright
R is for reading and running all right
E is for experience, extending my reach
N is for nursery school I want to teach
D is for dancing and digging each day
A is for ambitious, 'cause that's my way.

Tips for Busy Parents

Preteens like to think of themselves as independent. They prefer to do things for themselves, but swing from being totally responsible, mature individuals to pouting, demanding, immature brats. Their hormones are jumping, their temperaments volatile. If you turn your child into a reader now, you will make life easier for yourself and your child in the future.

1. *Put a book in your child's room.* This is tempting by tantalizing. If a new book is lying there, chances are your child will take a look at it.

2. *Talk about a book you enjoyed.* Find a book you enjoyed as a teenager or preteen. Read parts of it aloud to give your child the taste or flavor of the book. Read enough of it to entice your child to read the rest of it.

3. *Start your child on a new series.* Reading series books is like eating peanuts; you can't stop with one. When children read from a series, they know who the characters are, what to expect in the plot, and how it will probably turn out. They read fast, develop fluency, and increase their vocabulary. They pick up the reading habit. They will move on toward more sophisticated books as their reading habit grows and they find

reading is fun to do. *Harry Potter and the Sorceror's Stone* is a book both children and adults enjoy.

Did You Know . . .

- If adults in the home don't read, the children are not likely to pick up the reading habit.
- Children will read a book that a friend recommends more quickly than one an adult recommends.
- Something magical happens when a child reads the right book at the right time. If a child finds that a character in a book suffers from the same fears as her own, then she knows that she is not alone.
- A study of the scripts from eight TV shows popular with teens showed sentences averaging only seven words.
- Some TV shows are written on a fourth-grade reading level.
- Students who have the biggest vocabulary are the best readers. If you want to know how well a child will read, find out how many words he knows.
- Children learn to become better readers by reading. No matter what they read, the additional practice makes them better at what they do.
- Preteens and teenagers still need to hear someone read aloud. Find interesting bits in newspapers or magazines that you can read aloud.
- It is helpful to share reading secrets with children. Let them know that you sometimes skip a chapter, sneak a peek at the ending, or skip a word you don't know.
- Not all books are good books for everyone. Let your child develop his own taste for the types of books and magazines he reads.
- "I'm bored" usually doesn't mean that a child has nothing

to do, but that she isn't getting enough mental stimulation.

- Students who eat with their families have higher reading achievement than those who don't eat with family. They talk more and read better.
- Good books may not save the world, but they are one of the reasons the world is worth saving.

Chapter 10: A Final Word

As I was completing the manuscript for an earlier edition of this book, an article in my local newspaper made me think I had neglected an important part of reading aloud — helping a child learn to read or to become an avid reader. There is a special kind of joy that comes back to the one who reads aloud or serves as a tutor! I call it handing down the magic — the magic of knowing how to read.

The article describes a school volunteer project called Read Aloud that organizes more than 500 civic-minded people and business executives to visit individual classes in every school to read aloud for an hour and then to donate the books to the school. Even the mayor pulls up a child-sized chair to read aloud to avid listeners.

The teachers noticed that children were reading more books on their own than they ever had before the project started. One veteran teacher said, "I'm convinced it's due to Read Aloud." Furthermore, more volunteers were anxious to participate and they wanted to go to the schools more often. They enjoyed the process, too!

Several school and business partnerships now exist because word has spread that such programs make a difference in children's reading ability and have an additional benefit: Volunteer readers receive great personal satisfaction. One program's logo reads "Everybody Wins When Adults Read with Children."

Arthur Tannenbaum, founder of Everybody Wins, says, "The purpose of our organization is to motivate children to read when they are young so they become lifelong readers." Founded in 1991, Everybody Wins launched a Power Lunch program in which corporate volunteers share lunch and read with an elementary school child once a week. (For more information, see *www.everybodywins.org*.

Some people plan comprehensive programs to help students. For example, in 1981, Eugene Lang gave the sixth-grade graduation speech at P.S. 121, the elementary school he had attended more than fifty years earlier. Just before Lang began to give the graduation speech, the principal told him that 75 percent of the students would never finish high school. Lang was shocked and promised the sixty-one children sitting in front of him that he would give them a college scholarship if they graduated from high school.

Lang not only kept his promise, which continues as the "I Have a Dream" program, but he has expanded his vision to include other programs through the Eugene M. Lang Foundation.

Coca-Cola Valued Youth is a peer-tutoring program initiated in San Antonio, Texas, and duplicated in 150 schools across the United States, Brazil, England, and Puerto Rico. It is based on the philosophy that, if given a role of responsibility, students will rise to the level of expectation.

The program enlists middle and high school students who are struggling in school to become tutors for younger students also having trouble in school. Research shows that both the tutor and the taught gain markedly. An old saying, "You never really know a subject until you've taught it" proves to be true, and students who have struggled to learn seem to understand younger children who also struggle. Research and first-person reports show that the giver receives a great deal from the giving.

Volunteers who work with children learn the value of their work from the gratitude expressed in children's eyes and through their thanks. You can't give flowers to another without the scent of roses clinging to your hands.

Growing up on a farm kept me close to nature and the

basic qualities of life. It taught me that important things worth having are worth working for and worth waiting for. The trees I helped plant as a child are sturdy and huge now; they give shade to those who now farm the land. I remember the slender little saplings we planted and watered and nurtured and put stakes around so the cows wouldn't trample them. We took care of them because we cared about them. When I read *The Little Prince*, I find that Antoine de Saint-Exupéry said long ago that we are responsible for the things we raise. Our children are the most beautiful legacy we will ever have.

Michael Ende, in *The Neverending Story*, says that our fantasies and fairy-tale characters will die if we don't tell their stories. Our ability to imagine and to create a world of make-believe will not exist unless we keep it alive by passing it on to children. This is a part of our legacy to children; surely they deserve to hear the myths and legends that have been passed down to us. If our legends die, the world will be a less interesting place. And we will be less interesting people.

Each time you read a story to your child, you are planting a seed and nurturing it. Each time you use an activity that involves reading or writing, you are helping your child learn to love books. Congratulations on what you have done thus far. You've already learned that the joy you give returns to you a hundredfold; it keeps on growing. That's the beauty of planting seeds! I hope you raise a beautiful garden of readers to make the world a happier place.

SUREFIRE HITS BOOK LIST

BIRTH TO AGE 3

Alborough, Jez. *Tall*. Candlewick, 2005.

Cronin, Doreen. *Wiggle*. Illustrated by Scott Menchin. Atheneum, 2005.

Cronin, Doreen. *Duck for President*. Illustrated by Betsy Lewin. Scholastic, 2004.

Dillon, Leo and Diane. *Rap A Tap Tap*. Blue Sky Press, Scholastic, 2002.

Kuskin, Karla. *So, What's It Like to Be a Cat?* Illustrated by Betsy Lewin. Atheneum, 2005.

Kuskin, Karla. *Toots the Cat*. Illustrated by Lisze Bechtold. Holt, 2005.

Martin, Jr, Bill. *Brown Bear, Brown Bear, What Do You See?* Illustrated by Eric Carle. Holt, 1995.

Milich, Zoran, *City 1 2 3*. Kids Can Press, 2005.

Milord, Susan. *Love That Baby*. Houghton, 2005.

Peters, Lisa Westberg. *Cold Little Duck, Duck, Duck*. Illustrated by Sam Williams. HarperCollins, 2005.

Pomerantz, Charlotte. *The Piggy in the Puddle*. Illustrated by James Marshall. Simon & Schuster, 1989.

Roth, Carol. *The Little School Bus*. Illustrated by Pamela Paparone. North-South Books, 2002.

Sendak, Maurice. *Pierre: A Cautionary Tale in Five Chapters and a Prologue*. HarperCollins, 1991.

Shannon, George. *White Is for Blueberry*. Illustrated by Laura Dronzek. Greenwillow, 2005.

Wells, Rosemary. *My Kindergarten*. Introduction by Bernice E. Cullinan. Hyperion, 2004.

Yaccarino, Dan. *The Birthday Fish*. Holt, 2005.

Yolen, Jane. *How Do Dinosaurs Say Goodnight?* Illustrated by Mark Teague. Blue Sky Press, Scholastic, 2003.

Yolen, Jane. *How Do Dinosaurs Eat Their Food?* Illustrated by Mark Teague. Blue Sky Press, Scholastic, 2005.

AGES 3–5

Ahlberg, Allan. *The Children Who Smelled a Rat*. Illustrated by Katharine McEwen. Candlewick, 2005.

Araki, Mie. *Kitten's Big Adventure*. Gulliver, Harcourt, 2005.

Arnold, Todd. *Hi! Fly Guy*. Cartwheel Books, Scholastic, 2005.

Berenzy, Alix. *Sammy: The Classroom Guinea Pig*. Holt, 2005.

Brett, Jan. *Honey . . . Honey . . . Lion! A Story from Africa*. Putnam, 2005.

Calmenson, Stephanie, *Kindergarden Kids: Riddles, Rebuses, Wiggles, Giggles, and More!* Illustrated by Melissa Sweet. HarperCollins, 2005.

Cordsen, Carol Foskett. *The Milkman*. Illustrated by Douglas B. Jones. Dutton, 2005.

de Paola, Tomie. *Hide and Seek All Week*. Penguin, 2001.

Eastman, P. D. *Are You My Mother?* Random House, 1960.

Ehlert, Lois. *Leaf Man*. Harcourt, 2005.

Galdone, Paul. *The Three Bears*. Houghton Mifflin, 2000.

Gantos, Jack. *Best in Show for Rotten Ralph*. Illustrated by Nicole Rubel. Farrar, 2005.

Gretz, Susanna. *Riley and Rose in the Picture*. Candlewick, 2005.

Gritz, Ona. *Tangerines and Tea: My Grandparents and Me*. Illustrated by Yumi Heo Abrams, 2005.

Haas, Jessie. *Jigsaw Pon*. Illustrated by Ying-Hwa Hu. Greenwillow, 2005.

Himler, Ronald. *Dancing Boy*. Illustrated by Ronald Himler. Star Bright, 2005.

Hoberman, Mary Ann. *You Read to Me, I'll Read to You: Very Short Mother Goose Tales to Read Together*. Illustrated by Michael Emberley. Little Brown, 2005.

——. *You Read to Me, I'll Read to You: Very Short Stories to Read Together*. Little Brown, 2003.

Juster, Norton. *The Hello, Goodbye Window*. Illustrated by Chris Raschka, di Capua. Hyperion, 2005.

Krauss, Ruth. *Bears*. Illustrated by Maurice Sendak. HarperCollins, 2005.

Lobel, Arnold. *Frog and Toad are Friends* (Series). HarperCollins, 1970.

Marshall, James. *Goldilocks and the Three Bears*. Penguin, 1998.

Mayer, Mercer. *There Are Monsters Everywhere*. Dial, 2005.

McClintock, Barbara. *Cinderella*. Scholasatic, 2005.

Moore, Clement Clarke. *The Night before Christmas*. Illustrated by Lisbeth Zwerger. Minedition, 2005.

Peck, Jan. *Way Up High in a Tall Green Tree*. Illustrated by Valeria Petrone. Simon, 2005.

Pelletier, Andrew T. *The Amazing Adventure of Bathman!* Illustrated by Peter Elwell. Dutton, 2005.

Perrault, Charles. *Cinderella*. Illustrated by Marcia Brown. Simon & Schuster, 1997.

Priceman, Marjorie. *Hot Air: The (Mostly) True Story of the Hot-Air Balloon Ride*. Atheneum, 2005.

Reichert, Amy. *While Mama Had a Quick Little Chat*. Illustrated by Alexandra Boiger. Jackson/Atheneum, 2005.

Rockwell, Anne. *Little Shark*. Illustrated by Megan Halsey. Walker, 2005.

Rodman, Mary Ann. *My Best Friend*. Illustrated by E. B. Lewis. Viking, 2005.

Rylant, Cynthia. *The High-Rise Private Eyes: The Case of the Desperate Duck*. Illustrated by Brian Karas. Greenwillow, 2005.

Taylor, Eleanor. *Beep, Beep, Let's Go!* Bloomsbury, 2005.

Willems, Mo. *Leonardo the Terrible Monster*. Hyperion, 2005.

——. *The Pigeon Loves Things That Go!* Hyperion, 2005.

——. *Time to Say Please*. Hyperion, 2005.

AGES 6–8

Banks, Lynee Reid. *The Fairy Rebel*. Delacorte Press, 1985.

Blume, Judy. *Tales of a Fourth Grade Nothing*. Penguin, 2003.

Brown, Jeff. *Stanley, Flat Again*. HarperCollins, 2003.

Byars, Betsy. *The SOS File*. Henry Holt, 2004.

Chaikin, Miriam. *Angel Secrets: Stories Based on Jewish Legend*. Illustrated by Leonid Gore. Holt, 2005.

Cleary, Beverly. *Henry Huggins*. HarperCollins, 1950.

Clements, Andrew. *Frindle*. Simon and Schuster, 1998.

Dahl, Roald. *The BFG*. Farrar, Straus, Giroux, 1982.

Dalgliesh, Alice. *Courage of Sarah Noble.* Simon & Schuster, 1991.

Danziger, Paula. *Amber Brown is Not a Crayon.* Scholastic, 1995.

Desimini, Lisa. *Trick or Treat: Smell My Feet!* Blue Sky Press, Scholastic, 2005.

Fleischman, Sid. *The Whipping Boy.* HarperCollins, 2003.

Gannett, Ruth Stiles. *My Father's Dragon.* Bantam Doubleday Dell, 2005.

George, Jean Craighead. *My Side of the Mountain.* Penguin, 2001.

Grimes, Nikki. *Danitra Brown, Class Clown.* Illustrated by E.B. Lewis, Amistad. HarperCollins, 2005.

Hoberman, Mary Ann. *Fathers, Mothers, Sisters, Brothers.* Little Brown, 1991.

Hurston, Zora Neale. *Lies & Other Tall Tales.* Adapted by Christopher Myers. HarperCollins, 2005.

Kyuchukov, Hristo. *A History of the Romani People.* Boyds Mills, 2005.

Lester, Julius. *The Old African.* Illustrated by Jerry Pinkney. Dial, 2005.

Lewis, J. Patrick. *Please Bury Me in the Library.* Illustrated by Kyle M. Stone. Gulliver, Harcourt, 2005.

Paschen, Elise, ed. *Poetry Speaks to Children.* Sourcebooks, 2005.

Prelutsky, Jack. *Read a Rhyme, Write a Rhyme.* Illustrated by Meilo So. Knopf, 2005.

Rockwell, Thomas. *How to Eat Fried Worms.* Random House, 1973.

Sacher, Louis. *Sideways Stories from Wayside School.* HarperCollins, 1985.

Scieszka, Jon. *The True Story of the 3 Little Pigs.* Illustrated by Lane Smith. Penguin, 1996.

Sierra, Judy. *Schoolyard Rhymes, Kids' Own Rhymes for Rope Skipping, Hand Clapping, Ball Bouncing, and Just Plain Fun.* Illustrated by Melissa Sweet. Knopf, 2005.

Snickett, Lemony. *A Series of Unfortunate Events.* HarperCollins, 1999.

Varmer, Hjordis. *Hans Christian Andersen: His Fairy Tale Life.* Illustrated by Lilian Brogger. Anansi, Groundwood, 2005.

White, E.B. *Charlotte's Web.* HarperCollins, 1974.

AGES 9–13

Bruchac, Joseph. *Whisper in the Dark.* Illustrated by Sally Wern Comport. HarperCollins, 2005.

Clements, Andrew. *Things Not Seen.* Penguin, 2002.

Clugston-Major, Chynna. *Queen Bee.* Scholastic, 2005.

Codell, Esme Raji. *Sahara Special.* Hyperion, 2003.

Creech, Sharon. *Replay.* HarperCollins, 2005.

Delaney, Joseph. *The Last Apprentice; Revenge of the Witch.* Illustrated by Patrick Arrasmith. Greenwillow, 2005.

Erdrich, Louise. *The Game of Silence.* HarperCollins, 2005.

Hiaasen, Carl. *Flush.* Knopf, 2005.

Krull, Kathleen. *Leonardo da Vinci.* Illustrated by Boris Kulikov. Viking, 2005.

Martin, Ann M. The Baby-Sitters Club: *Kristy's Great Idea.* Illustrated by Raina Telgemeier. Scholastic, 2005.

Perkins, Lynne Rae. *Criss Cross.* Greenwillow, 2005.

Pullman, Philip. *The Scarecrow and His Servant.* Illustrated by Peter Bailey. Knopf, 2005.

Rowling, J.K. The Harry Potter Series. Arthur A. Levine, Scholastic Books, 2005.

Smith, Jeff. *Bone*. Scholastic, 1991.

Stauffacher, Sue. *Harry Sue*. Knopf, 2005.

Stephenson, Lynda. *Dancing with Elvis*. Eerdman, 2005.

CHILDREN'S MAGAZINES

Ages Four to Eight

Highlights for Children. Highlights for Children, Inc., P.O. Box 269, Columbus, OH 43272-0002. (800) 848-8922, www.highlights.com

Chickadee. The Young Naturalist Foundation, 35 Riviera Drive Unit 17, Markham Ontario L3R 8N4 Canada. (800) 387-4379. www.ows@owlkids.com

Ladybug: The Magazine for Young Children. Cricket Magazine Group, P.O. Box 7433, Red Oak, IA 51591-2434. (800) 827-0227. www.cricketmag.com

Owl: The Discovery Magazine for Children. The Young Naturalist Foundation, 35 Riviera Drive Unit 17, Markham Ontario L3R 8N4 Canada. (800) 387-4379. www.ows@owlkids.com

Ranger Rick. National Wildlife Federation, 8925 Leesburg Pike, Vienna, VA 22184-0001. (703) 790-4000. www.nwf.org/nwf/rrick.

Sesame Street Magazine. Sesame Street Magazine, P.O. Box 55518, Boulder, CO 80328-5518. www.ctw.org

Spider: The Magazine for Children. Cricket Magazine Group, P.O. Box 7433, Red Oak, IA 51591-2434. (800) 827-0227. www.cricketmag.com

Your Big Backyard. Your Big Backyard, P.O. Box 2038, Harian, IA 51593-0017. (800) 611-1599. www.nwf.org/nwf/ybby.com

Ages Eight to Twelve

American Girl. Pleasant Company Publications, Inc. 8400 Fairway Place, P.O. Box 62986, Middleton, WI 53562-0190. (800) 845-0005. www.americangirl.com

Boys Life. Boy Scouts of America, P.O. Box 152350, Irving, TX 75015-2079. (972) 580-2000. www.bsa.scouting.org/mags/boyslife.com

Cobblestone. Cobblestone Publishing, Inc., 30 Grove Street, Suite C, Peterborough, NH 03458. (603) 924-7209. www.cobblestonepub.com

Guideposts for Kids. Guideposts for Kids, 39 Seminary Hill Road Carmel, NY 10512-1999

Muse. Muse, P.O. Box 7468, Red Oak, IA 51591-0468. www.muse.com

National Geographic World. National Geographic Society, P.O. Box 98018, Washington, DC 20090-8018. (800) 368-2728. www.nationalgeographic. com

Nickelodeon. Nickelodeon, P.O. Box 11243, Des Moines, IA 50350.

Nintendo Power. Nintendo of America Inc., 4820 150th Avenue NE, Redmond, WA 98052.

Odyssey. Cobblestone Publishing, Inc., 7 School Street, Peterborough, NH 03458. (800) 821-0115. www.cobblestonepub.com

Sports Illustrated for Kids. Sports Illustrated for Kids, 820 Tom Martin Drive, Birmingham, AL 35211. (800) 992-0196. www.sikids.com

Time for Kids. Time & Life Building, 1271 Avenue of the Americas, New York, NY 10020-1393. (800) 777-8600. www.timeforkids.com

Zillions. Zillions Subscription Department, P.O. Box 54861, Boulder, CO 80321-4861. (800) 234-2078. www.zillions.com